HOW TO START A PODCAST

P TEAGUE

CONTENTS

1. The Joys of Podcasting   1
2. From Radio to Podcasts   13
3. How to Start Podcasting   23
4. Podcasting Equipment   45
5. Launching Your Podcast   63
6. Podcast Practicalities   74
7. Recording & Editing Your Podcast   98
8. Podcast Presentation Tips   110
9. Refining the Podcast Process   131
10. Podcast Interview Essentials   149
11. Accelerate Your Podcast   179
12. Growing Your Podcast Audience   194
13. Podcasting Next Steps   205
14. What Next?   213

About the Author   219

1

THE JOYS OF PODCASTING

Setting up my podcast is the single best thing I've done since starting to work online in 2001. It's fun, engaging, addictive and absorbing. One minute I can be sitting at the desk in my small study in Cumbria, recording my thoughts into my desktop computer. Within the hour, people all over the world can be listening to my content, then sharing and commenting on it on social media. That's more powerful than anything I was able to deliver during my 18-year career in the BBC working as a radio presenter, journalist and producer.

To achieve this remarkable feat of broadcasting, I don't need a team of scriptwriters and engineers. There's no need for a studio or a big radio mast; in the 21st Century this can all be done from the comfort of your own home and you don't need any special training or qualifications to do it. If you're happy to speak into a microphone and you've got some basic web skills – nothing more challenging than being able to make a listing on eBay or post on Facebook – then you really do have the prerequisites to podcast.

Add to that an almost obsessive passion about your

subject - and believe me, there really is no topic too obscure to find a podcast audience - then you have everything you need to set up your own show. If there's one sense I want to leave you with by the time you finish reading this book, it's that you can start a podcast, with virtually no expense and zero experience, and before long you too can be sharing your show with an international audience.

I worked in radio broadcasting for many years with the BBC and I've published well over 400 individual podcast episodes at the time of writing this book. I've built my entire career around communicating through words and audio, and now I want to share that experience and passion with you.

I'm hoping you're here because you can't wait to set up your own show and start sharing it with the world. If so, you're in the right place. Let's get started with the basics.

Before you read on ...

If at any point you're reading this book and you think to yourself: *I wish he'd put a weblink in there,* then worry not. Weblinks in ebooks and paperbacks are horrible to manage, so I have placed every single weblink connected with this book – and a lot of extras which I don't mention – on the accompanying website at PaulTeague.net/POD. So that's it; one weblink to rule them all. It also means I can add cool new stuff in future months.

Why should you start a podcast?

We all have different reasons for wanting to podcast. Hopefully, there's a topic which you feel passionate about, that's always the best place to start. As a rule, it needs to be the sort of thing that you can talk about, read about and think about for hours on end without getting bored. Is there something like that in your life?

The reason I ask is because you're going to know every inch of that topic by the time you hit episode 100. How will you feel about your subject by the time you reach episode 500? If that prospect excites you, rather than frightens you, you probably have a great contender for your podcast's subject matter.

The truth is, unless you get very lucky, you will probably not make money for some time when you start podcasting. It's best to base a show on an interest that you're passionate about, rather than as a route to fast and massive riches; that doesn't happen to most people. However, it certainly doesn't mean that you can't make *some* money from your podcast. I'll be telling you all about that later in this book.

When I launched Self-Publishing Journeys, these were my aims:

1) To speak to other self-published authors and learn from their experiences.
2) To promote a paid self-publishing course through the podcast.
3) To promote third-party products on the podcast website from which I take a small commission.

I achieved all of those objectives in the early days of the podcast, but it didn't take too long until I'd changed my course. I soon discovered that there's much more to a podcast than making money. Podcast bring all sorts of hidden benefits which I'd never have realised if I hadn't started the journey in the first place:

1) Podcasts are superb for networking – my podcast has

enabled me to speak to authors who are much more successful than I am and therefore give me a personal, 1-1 masterclass with them for free.

2) I have connected with other authors and editors who have enhanced my writing life through their skills and assistance. My two collaborative writing ventures came as a result of my podcast and I found two editors through my show.

3) My podcast gave me the credibility to do things that were far beyond my level of success. I have represented The Alliance of Independent Authors, presented to delegates at The Society of Authors, and shared the stage three times with bestselling authors at Amazon UK events.

4) I've made some great friends in my industry. I can attend writing events and people recognise me from my voice.

5) I've been paid for consultation by podcast listeners, without me ever having to sell it as a service. People come to me; I don't have to sell anything to them.

I posted my first blog post in 2009 and have blogged on and off for the past decade, without consistency or any particular strategy. I can tell you that in two decades of online working, and having spent all those years in radio, I have never been engaged in any activity which connected so intimately and closely with the audience. Podcasting is remarkable. It's my favourite way of creating content and communicating with fellow enthusiasts in my chosen niche, which is all rather convenient, because it's just like running my own radio station – without the engineers, the hassles of a day-job or the boss shouting at me down the telephone because I played a Toyah CD and he doesn't like Toyah. And yes, that did really happen.

What is a podcast anyway?

I'm hoping that if you're reading this book, you're already a listener to podcasts. If you're reading this and you've never listened to a podcast before, I suggest you make that your next step before you read on any further. Please make sure you've found some shows that you enjoy and spend some time listening to them. It would be very unwise to start your own podcast before you've got a firm grip on what they are and how you access them as a listener.

It's important that you do this as basic homework because it's good to have an idea of what you're aiming for in your own show. We're going to have to think about show format, the number of presenters who will anchor the show, whether to include jingles, episode release intervals and all sorts of other factors. You need to have a good idea of what works for you personally before you launch off into space with your own show. Remember, I want you to succeed at this.

I tend to avoid getting too academic about things, preferring to leave that to the professors and lecturers. Here's my best shot at a definition of podcasts, using Wikipedia as my inspiration and guide:

Podcasts are digital audio files which are released in an episodic series. They can be listened to on mobile phones, desktop computers, laptops and tablets. The best way to consume them is via a subscription which allows new episodes to be automatically delivered to the listener on publication.

It's a bit like radio, only it's not live and you listen on your phone or computer. The other big deal from my – and your – point of view, is that anybody can do it. You don't need to be a company, a brand, a corporation or anything posh like that to start a podcast.

I like to use the word *democratisation* when referring to podcasts. In simple terms, that means you and I can do this, using only our phone or laptop, from the comfort of our kitchen or living room.

Podcast examples

Even if you don't listen to podcasts you may have heard of some of the biggies in the media. Podcasts have gone mainstream, they're the 'must-have' for every business because they connect with audiences in a way that wasn't possible before.

The award-winning *Serial* podcast is probably one of the most widely talked about podcasts in recent years. It combined investigative journalism with great storytelling in order to tell a true story over the course of a single season.

This American Life is a hugely popular podcast in the United States with – wait for it – around one million listeners downloading each episode. That's a bigger audience than most radio stations have. And you can replicate that from your front room.

You will, no doubt, have your own favourites. You're only going to see more podcasts like these, not fewer. There are some very good reasons for this too.

Podcasting boom time

If you subscribe to Netflix or any other on-demand TV series you'll already know how great it is being able to access the TV that you want to watch, 24/7, without schedulers placing adverts in your way or forcing you to wait a week between episodes.

When I was a kid, I actually gave up horse riding lessons

because they clashed with a TV series I was desperate to see. Now, no jokes about my age please, but in those days, we didn't have videos or hard drives; if you missed it, you missed it.

They were the dark ages of TV. Those of you who binge-watch series will know what great joy comes from watching TV on your own terms.

Now think of radio, which has been slower to catch up.

You have to tune in a radio, which sometimes catches and often loses the signal, only to listen to some self-opinionated presenter who forces their choice of music upon you, speaks over the intros and outros, and then decides what the topic of conversation is for the day. Now, don't get me wrong, that's how I made my living for years. But that model is long past its sell-by date, and that's where podcasts come in.

Podcasts are Netflix for the ears. You get to choose the topic, the presenter – or presenters – and the time and place that you will listen. Can't get to sleep and want to listen at three o'clock in the morning? No problem with a podcast. Like the topic, but hate the presenter? Just find another podcast on the same topic until you find a presenter that you like. I'm going to use that word again – *democratisation*. That's what has happened with podcasts. The listener is firmly in the driving seat, but so is the presenter. The listener gets exactly what they want when they want it, and however many times they want to listen to it. People like me and you get to take a piece of the action too. I've seen and studied radio station listening figures for more hours than I care to remember and I can tell you that I reach more people through my home-made podcast than I used to reach on the teatime show on a local radio station which shall remain nameless.

Podcasts are all around you too. We're all aware of Apple Podcasts, the ruler of them all, but Google also has a podcast channel now (more about that very important move later), and so does Spotify. These aren't tiny operators; when Google moves in, you know something big is brewing.

Podcasting benefits

I mentioned earlier that podcasts are the best thing I've done in my business, bar none. Podcasts, in my opinion, are better than blogging, yet the way I'm going to tell you to set up your podcast will make it every bit as good as blogging, just a little easier to maintain.

If you asked me to pick the one best thing about podcasts, I'd say it's *connection*. There's something about having a podcast host's voice in your ear that creates a familiar and intimate relationship with them, more than a blog post or book could ever do. When you listen to my podcast you hear my voice, warts and all. You hear me as I speak naturally, chatting only to you, directly in your ears via your earbuds. You can tell if I'm being phoney, you get to decide if you love or hate my voice, if you like me or hate me, or if you think I'm talking non-stop rubbish or wall-to-wall pure gold. It's like having a friend in the room. If people connect with you on a podcast, they tend to become very dedicated to your show.

I'm a huge consumer of podcasts, I listen to them when-ever I'm walking or running alone, and they keep me company late at night if I can't sleep. At the time of writing this sentence, I have 29 podcast subscriptions on my phone, and I have already consumed four different shows on this day alone. I have been listening to three of those podcasts for more than four years. I have met several of the hosts of those podcasts, and I am responsible for three of those podcasts being set up in the first place. Now, how's that for connection?

Why podcasts work

There's a saying in business that for prospects and customers to buy from you they need to *know, like and trust* you. Ring any bells? That's exactly what you get from a podcast, once you've established that intimate connection with the audience. They get to know you and, if they decide they like you, they'll soon get a sense of your authenticity and learn to trust you as a great source of knowledge, tips, advice and information.

This is where podcasts work best. The lovely thing about them is that if people don't like what you're doing, they just tend to unsubscribe and find something that they like better. No moaning, no trolling, no hassle; they just move on and leave your show alone for the most part. But if they decide they like you? You might have just found a friend for life!

Podcasts as a hobby

Before we start to get our hands dirty, I want to stress one very important principle. You may wish to start a podcast as a hobby because you're passionate about a particular topic and you just can't get enough of it. I want to emphasise from the outset that it's absolutely fine to do that. You can start a podcast and never make a penny from it, and in some respects that's often the best motivation to get started. Many podcasters have found that doing just that has brought sponsorship and financial offers their way, and if that happens to you, I'd like to be the first to congratulate you. It's an important point though; you do not have to make any money, sell any products or sign up clients to any course or service if you have a podcast. If you just love your subject, that's fine.

As we progress through this book, you'll constantly hear me referring to podcasts as a business. If you're a hobby podcaster, just take what's useful and leave what's not. Even if you are a hobby podcaster, it's still good to see how best to set things up. But when it comes to your show, follow the set-up process, launch your podcast and just enjoy sharing all that wonderful knowledge and passion for your subject. And if you ever do decide to ramp things up, just turn back to the relevant chapters and you'll know exactly how to take things forward.

Your podcast's purpose

Why are you starting your podcast? Seriously, what's the point of it? I don't mean to be rude, but I hope you're not doing it just because it's more interesting than watching paint dry.

It's important to have a clear idea of why you're setting up your show. It doesn't matter hugely what that purpose is, but it's good to be clear. For example, the purpose of my self-publishing podcast diary is *to allow new and aspiring indie authors to listen in on my self-publishing author journey in order to share what I'm doing, pass on tips and techniques, and let them know that they're not alone as new and inexperienced writers.*

The purpose of my self-publishing interview episodes is *to connect with indie authors who are at a similar stage to me – or more advanced than me – in order to share their writing journeys and to learn – and share – their best tips and techniques.*

Finally, the purpose of my crypto podcast was *to collate, share and discuss the most important weekly developments in cryptocurrencies in order to educate myself and the new-to-crypto audience.*

You'll notice that sometimes my purpose is self-centred. One of the benefits of running your own podcast is that you can connect with people who are much further ahead than you are and a lot more experienced. Your show can be an excellent channel for securing no-cost consultancy from industry titans. I learn all the time from my podcast guests, whatever stage in their career they've reached. As well as providing what I hope is a useful service to other writers, I also get a lot of benefits myself.

Try writing a sentence like my examples above. All of this will help to clarify your purpose and desired podcast outcomes.

Podcasting's hi-tech future

There are some technical reasons why you need to pay attention to podcasts. Do you have a voice assistant yet? If the answer is no, think again. If you have Windows 10, you have Cortana on your desktop computer. That's voice-activated. If you have an Apple device, you have Siri. Perhaps you have a Google Assistant or Alexa or something else in your house that's voice-activated.

This concept is known as 'voice-first' and it's only going to grow bigger and more pervasive in our lives.

Voice is big and it's going to grow more dominant. And here's the kicker: Google is now evolving its search engine algorithms to take account of the changes voice-first is making in our lives. Where once we typed words into a little box on the Google search page, in future, we'll just speak the words. Only, when we speak, we use different words to when we type, and Google is already adjusting for this.

Strategically, Google is increasingly going to be indexing voice-based search results. That means your keyword-rich, SEO-friendly podcast episodes are going to start appearing in Google search results. Who do you know who runs their own podcast? Are your business competitors running their own podcast? The answer to those questions is probably no, which means podcast hosts have first-mover advantage in the brave new world of Google's audio-first search results.

Key points

- Podcasting and audio are experiencing a boom time. Now is a great time to get started.
- You can podcast for fun or you can podcast with the aim of making money. It doesn't matter if you treat it as a hobby or a business, but it is best to be passionate about your subject.
- Podcasts are much more effective than blogs for engaging with your audience.
- It's best to be clear about your podcast's purpose before you start work on your new show.

2

FROM RADIO TO PODCASTS

If you just want to get on with the 'how-to' element of podcasting, you have my permission to skip this chapter and head directly for Chapter 3. However, if you're the type of person who wouldn't buy a car without knowing its service history first, you'll want to read on. It would be rude of me to write a book and not tell you who I am and why I'm suggesting to you that I can help you to get your first podcast underway. After all, you wouldn't take medical advice from a car mechanic or dental advice from a dog groomer, so why should you listen to me when it comes to podcasting advice? This is the chapter in the book where I convince you that this isn't just a theoretical book, or one where I assembled all the good bits from other peoples' books. I know what I'm talking about because I've been doing this professionally for over a quarter of a century now.

I've been speaking into microphones since I was ten years old. Little did I know when I recorded my pretend radio shows into the cassette player at primary school that it would eventually lead to a career in broadcasting with the BBC and ultimately, to me hosting my own podcasts.

In those early days, I would mimic what I'd heard on the radio and try to replicate it via a cheap microphone and compact cassettes which had a terrible habit of slurring and getting chewed up. Those childhood attempts at broadcasting could only be heard by an audience located in the immediate proximity of the small speaker that was mounted into the cassette player.

Fast forward over forty years, and these days I can record my podcast episodes on a handheld phone that's about one-twentieth of the size of a cassette player and within minutes it can be listened to by an audience throughout the world. No jamming or slurring either, unless the presenter is having a bad day. My podcast statistics inform me that I have listeners in the US, Canada, New Zealand, Australia, France, Spain, India, and even the occasional download in China, Russia, Brazil and Argentina. That's remarkable for a guy like me who grew up trying to nurse chewed up compact cassettes back from the dead, and who once had to broadcast with the help of the BBC to reach an audience beyond my front room. These days I can record a show at my kitchen table, and it can be downloaded onto phones and laptops throughout the world in a matter of minutes, using only basic equipment and with not an engineer in sight.

This is the true democratisation of audio and it means that if you have a burning desire to get your content out into the world, you can do so today, using equipment that you probably already own. In this book, I'm going to tell you exactly how it's done and get you started on your own broadcasting journey, even if you've never been near a microphone before.

My broadcasting background

It was a natural progression from cassette recorders to a career in radio. I never wanted to be on the TV, it was always about audio for me. That might seem strange as TV always seems more glamorous to most people. But that never bothered me, I was radio through and through. TV is a different beast, requiring lots of messing about with cameras, lighting, framing shots and getting things just right. In radio, you went on air and you were directly through to your audience. There's no fuss, no nonsense, you press the switch to go live and you're in cars, kitchens, living rooms and cafés immediately. I always loved that directness about voice-only broadcasts, and it's continued with podcast creation.

I progressed from creating rough and ready shows on cassette recorders to being a teenager who began to write and contribute to my secondary school magazine, eventually setting up a mobile disco with a school friend at the age of sixteen. Two years after, I was given the opportunity to stand in for one of my dad's friends on a local hospital radio station. It was a half-hour show, with speech and music, and I was terrified. It was live, no dry-runs, and I still have the script and cassette recording of my first ever broadcast. And no, you can't hear it. I can't believe how young and nervous I sound when I listen back to it. But I'd caught the bug, I loved it and wanted more.

I applied to colleges based on their having student radio stations, what I actually studied was always secondary to the burning ambition to start a career in broadcasting. It took me nine years to land a job in radio. I broadcast live radio shows on University Radio Bailrigg at the University of Lancaster for the four years of my teaching degree, mostly on Saturday mornings. I still have show tapes. We had amazing fun making those shows.

When I left college and began teaching, I continued to keep my foot in the door at the university's student radio station, broadcasting shows on Sunday evenings. I'd had an early skirmish with the BBC in my final year at college, but I messed up the interview and was ill-prepared for it. Eventually, they gave me a job at the age of 27, after I left teaching to take a Postgraduate Diploma in Radio & TV Journalism in Preston in 1990.

From 1991-2010 I was employed by the BBC, an achievement of which I'm incredibly proud. It took many years of commitment to land that job and I enjoyed a wonderful broadcasting career with the corporation. I must have broadcast thousands of hours of live radio. I've interviewed politicians, celebrities, rock stars and many hundreds of 'ordinary' people with remarkable stories. 'Ordinary' people usually have the best stories, by the way. I've presented breakfast shows, phone-in shows, gardening shows and religious shows covering all sorts of topics and issues. I've done hard-hitting journalistic interviews, delicate emotional interviews, painful interviews with unwilling guests and – perhaps the most challenging of them all – teasing full sentences from children.

I've recorded interviews under enormous time pressure, dealt with legal hot potatoes live on air, managed every technical nightmare that you can think of and even interviewed a gangster. He was even so good as to reassure me that people like him tended not to seek out people like me. Thank goodness for that!

So why am I telling you all this? After all, you're not interviewing me for a job. There are two reasons for me sharing this information about my broadcasting background. Firstly, to reassure you that this is not an academic or theoretical book. I've been in the trenches. The BBC paid me for eighteen years to put my voice on the radio and coach other people on how to do it. Secondly, after all that time broadcasting, I'd like to think I have a reasonable idea of what I'm talking about by now. I can share everything I've learnt from many years stuck in front of a microphone and a lot of those tips will be insider secrets, the type of knowledge you'd only get if you'd worked in broadcasting. And the BBC is no amateur outfit; they know their stuff.

My podcasting experience

I took voluntary redundancy from the BBC in 2010 because my work had evolved from radio broadcasting to working on the web. In my later career, I was learning how to live-stream radio broadcasts and place audio files onto servers so that they could be accessed all over the world. My web team and I won an international Webby Award for our online work, for making early and innovative use of audio and video technology. We even got a trip to New York on expenses in order to pick up the award.

It makes perfect sense then that, at some point, my radio and web careers would merge to create a new, leaner and much more modern hybrid. Podcasting was the natural culmination of all that experience, but it took me a little while to get there.

My first foray into the world of podcasting was with a test interview in 2009. It was early days for podcasting back then and nowhere near as easy as it is now to set up and sustain an online show. I recorded an interview with a UK-based Multi-Level Marketer and that episode was released in July 2009, a year before I moved on from the BBC. It was recorded on Skype and probably edited using the same software that I'll be recommending to you later in this book.

So why didn't I carry on podcasting? Well, I realised immediately that sustaining that level of output was going to take some commitment and I wasn't certain I was up to it at that time. Fast forward to April 2016 and I finally bit the bullet. I launched my Self-Publishing Journeys podcast (at PaulTeague.net/podcast) in April 2016 and I have never missed recording a weekly episode to the present date. In addition, I set up and ran a second podcast for a year in 2018, and this show ran for 74 episodes. At the time of writing this book, I have produced, recorded and released over 400 podcast episodes. That takes some commitment, which is why I shied away from podcasting when I first tried it out in 2009.

My training experience

The last part of my resumé is my teaching and training experience. While I was working hard to break into radio, I trained and worked as a teacher. As an author and digital marketer, I now work with creatives and local businesses in order to teach them about websites, social media, podcasting, e-learning products, webinars and everything else that you can do on the internet.

As a trainer, I specialise in making technical subjects simple, accessible and understandable. There's nothing worse than talking to somebody in the IT department at work and they proceed to overwhelm you with all sorts of technical gobbledegook that you simply don't need to know.

I've taught hundreds of local businesses 1-1 and many more via webinars and online training materials about how to do this stuff. I make it simple, navigate through the tech speak and nonsense to tell training clients what they need to know, what they can ignore and how to get started fast. That's the approach I will be bringing to this book. I will not be attempting to amaze you with my technical prowess. Instead, I'll set you on a clear path to starting a podcast and releasing your first episodes as fast as possible. I'll also be passing on lots of great broadcasting tips along the way.

How I can help to get you podcasting fast

Hopefully, I've managed to convince you that I ought to know what I'm talking about. I hope that you're raring to go by now. However, I am definitely not an audio engineer or an acoustics professional, so when it comes to getting all fancy with microphones that are the size of a tennis racket and recording environments that look like the Sydney Opera House, I'm not your man. But that's for a very good reason; you simply don't need any of that stuff to get started in podcasting.

When I started my podcast, there was a statistic doing the rounds that the average podcast didn't last for more than ten episodes. Now, I don't know the source of that statistic or even how current it is, but it serves as a useful baseline regardless of where it came from. The chances are you won't last beyond ten episodes. I repeat that statistic not to put you off, but to focus your mind on what's most important about this business. It is not setting up a fancy studio, posing with an expensive microphone and imagining you're a hotshot presenter at the top of your game. The biggest challenge when you start podcasting is going to be starting and sustaining your new show. Focus on the show first, then get fancy with the equipment once you get bitten by the bug and you're sure you're going to keep it up.

There's another phrase I love when it comes to starting a new hobby: *all the gear and no idea.* Don't be that podcaster. I'm going to guide you through everything you need to start, sustain and enjoy podcasting. I'm going to show you how to do it on the smallest budget possible. I'm also going to give you so many tips to make the process manageable that it will give you the best chance possible of beating my own output of over 400 podcast episodes and counting. I really want you to succeed in this journey; believe me, expensive kit is definitely *not* the most important factor in that process.

How this will work

It's time we got started! As you can probably tell already, I'm going to give short shrift to a lot of the nonsense surrounding podcasting. What follows in this book is a step-by-step, simple and cheap process to get your first podcast up and running. I've done this before too. I set up a corporate podcast in my home county in the UK which receives thousands of downloads and is more successful than any of us ever expected. I coached a colleague in how to manage the podcast and he now handles the entire process on his own and loves every moment of it. As a former newspaper reporter, he's found a new lease of life as a podcaster and I love seeing the satisfaction he gets from it. I taught him all the processes I'm going to share with you in the following chapters; this stuff works.

I have also coached author friends on how to set up their own podcasts and it has been gratifying to see that they've been able to work through the notes cobbled together during our chats to get their own products recorded and launched using the techniques I taught them.

It's high time I wrote all this down and shared it with a wider audience.

Bootstrapping podcast principles

I want you to get podcasting as fast as possible. I want to remove all the technical hurdles, the decisions, the geekery and the confusion. My aim is to lead you towards releasing your first episodes in as short a time as possible, telling you what's important and what's not, and removing all the barriers that might get in your way. To enable us to take that journey together, I want to introduce you to a concept known as *bootstrapping*.

Now, I'm a big fan of bootstrapping, it's the way I built my Facebook software when I was an internet marketer and the technique I used to build up my writing business. In simple terms, it means we don't spend money that we haven't earned. It's a solid business principle and will keep any extravagant excesses firmly in place. Now, if you've got loads of money to spare and you can afford to blow £500 on a microphone for a podcast that you might never get around to launching, by all means, be my guest. But if you're on a tight budget and you really need to get your podcast up and running without spending a fortune, then listen up.

I'm going to show you how you can get started for the price of a Logitech headset – presently about £30. Seriously, a podcast needn't cost any more than that to set up. I can even tell you where to get free hosting for your episodes and free editing software, though those recommendations will come with some cautionary notes.

When we bootstrap a business, we put as little of our own money in upfront and we adopt a principle that the business has to earn money before we spend it. Instead of encouraging you to go out and spend a fortune on equipment that you don't need – and it's certainly possible to do this if you really want to – I'm going to encourage you along the nursery slopes getting things underway quickly so that you're in a position to take your podcast message out into the world and begin the process of sharing your knowledge, your products or your services. We'll be doing that without breaking the bank.

Key points

- Avoid *all the gear and no idea.* Make sensible decisions about the tools you use when you start podcasting.
- Adopt bootstrapping principles – don't spend money on your podcast that you don't have. Wait until you have launched your first episodes before increasing your ambitions too much.
- I've worked in radio for almost two decades and have produced and recorded over 400 podcast episodes, so you're in safe hands as I guide you through this process.

3

HOW TO START PODCASTING

Decisions, decisions, decisions. That's what you're going to have to make lots of before you start recording that lovely voice of yours. Unfortunately, you can't just leap into podcast land with your eyes closed and if you do, without any forethought or planning, you're likely to come a cropper.

In this part of the book, I'll walk you through some of the choices you'll have to make before you get started. It won't take long, and it'll help to make sure your podcast doesn't fizzle out after a couple of episodes. I want you to avoid the phenomenon of *podfade* and inoculate your new venture against joining the legions of former podcasters who launched into their new show with naive enthusiasm, only to start spluttering after a couple of weeks because they hadn't thought things through properly. It's worth taking an hour or so with a cup (or glass!) of whatever takes your fancy to get these items bottomed out. After that, we can start to discuss the exciting stuff that will make you feel like a real broadcaster: microphones, recording software and technical set-ups.

What it takes

I'm sorry to have to tell you this, but podcasting over a long period of time takes perseverance, grit, commitment and planning. If you'd asked me if I thought I would make it to four years of podcasting and never miss a week of recording, I'd have been doubtful. There have been many occasions during that time when I really didn't feel like it. Perhaps I was too tired, I didn't feel well or – in the case of my diary episodes – I'd had such a bad week that I didn't really feel like sharing my depressing news. With my weekly accountability format, it can sometimes feel like I'm jumping into a boxing ring with an opponent who I know is going to make it hurt.

Somehow, I manage to keep dragging myself up by my bootstraps and getting those episodes recorded. It's important to hit that regular release schedule – your listeners won't thank you if you promise them an episode and you don't deliver.

Sometimes, it can feel like you're only speaking to a handful of people and, in the middle of a busy or hectic week, you'll ask yourself: *Why am I doing this?* Often you won't be able to come up with a good answer and you'll just have to carry on anyway.

Now, if all of this sounds like First World problems to you, you're absolutely right. But I can almost guarantee that if you're in this for the long term, you'll hit hurdles just like these. It's important to know *why* you're starting your podcast, how you will measure your success and ultimately, what do you want out of it?

If you're happy to release episodes to a handful of fellow enthusiasts, that's great. If you think you'll be a podcasting millionaire by the end of the week, that's probably an unrealistic expectation and you're setting yourself up for disappointment. I really hope that's your experience, but the evidence indicates it's unlikely.

Enthusiasm and love for your subject will always be good reasons to podcast. If you just have a passion that you want to share with the world, and you don't have ambitious financial targets or download numbers in your sights, then you probably have a good chance at sticking with this. Many a hobbyist podcaster started out in this way, then discovered that the accolades, sponsorships and listeners appeared as a by-product of doing a great job. There's no reason whatsoever why you shouldn't set out like the Terminator to obliterate all competition, generate millions of pounds in revenue and win multiple broadcasting awards, but that path is much less predictable and may result in disillusionment after a short time if the results don't come in fast enough.

Decide why you're doing this, set some realistic expectations, and I recommend that love for your topic and a desire to talk about it are two of your core motivations.

Selecting your audience & niche

Having got your podcasting purpose sorted out, it's time to move onto the all-important topic: *what* are you going to talk about? This is where I start discussing niches, a crucial concept to know about if you do any kind of work online. Niches need to be defined, refined and confined. Okay, I struggled with that last word, but it kind of makes sense, please bear with me.

Before I started working online, I truly believed a niche was the place in our living room where my dad stored a couple of books and my mum placed some of her ornaments. How little I knew. In business terms, a niche defines a product, a topic, interest or a service which meets the needs of a small and specialised group of customers or prospects. Niches are always better when they're clearly defined. It helps you attract the right people and repel the wrong ones.

Think of the topic of sport. That's a very broad definition. It includes football, rugby, tennis, bowls, badminton, fly fishing and who knows what other remarkable activities I've never heard of from all over the world. Now, let's niche that down even further. For each of those sports, we have professional, semi-professional and amateur. We have men's, women's, boys', girls' and mixed as well as numerous age categories within each gender definition. If I'm a 15-year-old boy who loves playing mixed doubles tennis, I may have a general interest in tennis as a sport, but I'm particularly interested in my specific niche. Niches are important, they really matter.

The rule of thumb on the internet is that you need to pick a narrow niche, then go really deep with it. That way you will appeal to people who have a very specific and keen interest in what you're doing. If you go too wide with your niche, you're likely to please some of the people all of the time, all of the people none of the time, but never please all of the people all of the time. It was the poet John Lydgate whose quote I paraphrased there by the way. Never let it be said that this book isn't educational.

I have defined my podcast as follows: *The Essential Weekly Podcast for New & Aspiring Indie Authors*. My show is very specifically aimed at inexperienced authors who want to self-publish. If you want to be traditionally published, it's not for you. If you're an experienced author who's doing well in your career, it's not for you. If you're about to begin self-publishing – or you just got started – mine is the perfect show for you. By defining my niche, I attract the right people and repel the wrong listeners.

Returning to my dodgy *defined, refined and confined* analogy, you need to define your niche, then refine it further and finally, confine your podcast topics to that specific area. Your listeners will thank you for it, because they know exactly what they're signing up for and you'll deliver it, week after week. By the way, I hope you're impressed with how I managed to justify the use of the word *confined* in that list, it took some doing.

To be fair, I could probably define my own niche even more precisely if I wanted to. I might add fiction or non-fiction to that definition. I might niche down further by genre, with thrillers or science fiction. The better defined the niche, the easier it will be to win and retain a dedicated audience. Go broad at your peril. Your audience is never everybody. If you ever hear yourself saying: *I like to think it appeals to everybody and anybody*, you've done it wrong. Please return to this section and read it again.

Listen to other industry podcasts

Having defined and clearly articulated your niche, it's time to see what else is out there. When I chose self-publishing as a topic, I already had lots of competitors who'd been around for several years. However, at the time I started my show, I had listened to many of those podcasts and mine grew out of a specific need that I had. There were some great podcasts available in my niche – I still listen to most of them – but they were too advanced for me at the time I started out. Nobody else was reflecting my experiences. They were telling me how they were earning thousands of dollars from book sales and I hadn't even sold my first book at the time. They were well-connected, knew how to do all the technical stuff, and were quite intimidating because they'd had so much success.

My podcast was born out of a desire to speak to new self-published authors who were in the trenches, publishing their first books, making their first sales, earning less than $100 per month, and often struggling to attain even those meagre levels. Although there were many podcasts available in my niche, I whittled down my topic to create a service that nobody – at the time – was providing.

There's very little point starting a podcast which is an exact replica of something that's already doing very well. In that scenario, you're entering into a competition. It's fine if you want to do that, but from a listener's point of view, what extra value are you adding to the topic? Sometimes, that extra value may just be you and your personal experience, and that's fine. But in that scenario, you're basing your podcast around personality, and you'd be best to have a platform already if you go down that route.

For instance, Richard Branson and Elon Musk are both very famous and successful businesspeople. If they both started business podcasts, we'd listen anyway, because of who they are. Now, you don't need to be a celebrity of their magnitude to go down the personality route, but I'd always advise that particular path if you already have an audience from another source: perhaps readers of a bestselling book, fans who bought your latest music release, and so on.

Outlining your podcast talking points

Having decided on your niche, I'd recommend taking it out for a spin. Write down ten topics that you could discuss for your first ten podcast episodes. You don't need to go into any detail, just a simple one-sentence outline for each episode is fine.

Now add ten more. Yes, seriously! The first ten will only take you to the point at which many podcasters experience *podfade*. We need to see if you have the impetus to shoot well beyond that. If the thought of coming up with twenty topics fills you with horror, it probably indicates that either you don't know your topic well enough or you've chosen the wrong niche, perhaps going too narrow with its definition. You have to give yourself sufficient scope for different topics.

This is a good test to make sure that you're setting out on the correct path; it's best you figure this out sooner rather than later. If you defined your topic too narrowly, expand it a little. If your podcast was going to be about wooden spade handles made in 1983, you may need to flex a little bit. Try expanding your niche to modern tools for vegetable gardening to give yourself more scope. By the way, although I was being tongue-in-cheek there, there's probably an audience for that topic. It's why I love podcasting so much; it doesn't matter how obscure your niche might seem, there's always somebody out there who's equally interested in your favourite subject.

Timeless or topical?

Having selected a great topic that's not too broad, and not ridiculously narrow, you need to decide if you're going for an evergreen model or a time-dependent format. An evergreen model is simply a format where the content is timeless and never dates. Both have advantages and disadvantages and it's well worth a few moments of your time familiarising yourself with the differences.

I'm a fan of the evergreen model. I have written seven non-fiction books before this one and they all dealt with internet-based topics. I used how-to screenshot images, showed exactly what to do in a step-by-step format, and life was sweet. Then Facebook, Twitter, LinkedIn and the rest changed the look and feel of their services, added a few features and removed others, and my books were obsolete. That's why this book has no images and no step-by-step how-to sequences. There's no point; that content will be dated in no time at all. This book is an evergreen book, the advice in it won't change for a long time. LinkedIn once changed the look of their website completely a couple of days after I'd updated one of my books; it made me want to cry.

In my own podcast, my author interviews are examples of evergreen content. Talking about how writers got started, what they write, what their tips are, is always interesting information. When authors make big strides in their careers, I sometimes record update interviews. But these podcast episodes have longevity, they're interesting any time you listen to them (or at least I hope they are!).

You may prefer a news format. My now defunct cryptocurrency podcast was that type of show. Each week I'd dig out the latest stories from the crypto scene, assemble them in a sensible order and share them with the world. That creates a great hook for listeners, but you may subsequently find that people don't listen to your older episodes.

It's worth noting here that people who love your podcast will listen to everything, however old it is. For people who enjoy your work, it's like finding a wonderful TV show that they can't get enough of. They devour your old content, even if it is dated; essentially, they're listening to you, it's *you* who they like, the content is secondary.

I have always mixed timeless and topical, with both my crypto podcast and my self-publishing podcast. I guess I like to have my cake and eat it. The crypto podcast was made up of a combination of weekly news updates, guest interviews and 'education' episodes, where we dug deep into particular topics, like security.

My self-publishing podcast features the weekly diary episodes which have, over time, created a wonderful record of my journey from new and aspiring writer to somebody who can now make a living from it. I hope that the back catalogue will help to encourage and inspire other authors. My interviews create evergreen entry points for people discovering my podcast. Both work effectively in their own way, but do give some thought to which option you will go for. Or, follow my examples, and do both. It's your show, you decide. And there we go with democratisation again.

Podcast titles, SEO & discoverability

It's time to ramp up the pace of your learning. First it was the concept of niches. Now it's the turn of SEO – search engine optimisation. This is a dark art and one which you need to have a grasp of before you get stuck in for real.

For the purposes of this explanation, I'm going to assume you use Google as your default search engine. When you enter the phrase 'dog food' into Google, you want and expect the search engine to come up with a list of dog food options in response to your query. If you get cat food, goat food (is that a thing?) or hamster food, you're going to be nonplussed. You may even be so angry it might have you asking whatever happened to that wonderful tool called Internet Explorer.

When you entered *dog food* into Google, you had a

search intent. You expected to find what you were looking for. So how will I find your podcast if I search on Google?

If I had called my podcast *The Paul Teague Show*, it would have died a fast and painful death. Not only does nobody know who I am (other than you, my friends and my family), that title says nothing about my topic. Nobody's typing *Paul Teague* into Google and even if they do, they're going to have to be pretty desperate to listen to a show that doesn't say what it's about.

Now, if I add a description to that title, we can start to make some headway. If my podcast is *The Paul Teague Show: your weekly look at the world of horticulture and gardening* things are suddenly making more sense. I think I may have just found myself another podcast topic, by the way!

The question to ask yourself when coming up with the name for your new show is: *if I were looking specifically for my show, what words would I type into Google in order to find it?*

If your podcast is about pizza, then the title needs to include that word. However, pizza is a very broad keyword, so you need to be more specific. Perhaps your show is about vegan pizzas, cooking pizzas, pizza delivery services or best, frozen pizzas. Be specific, or else we don't stand a chance of finding you.

Your podcast format

Every radio and TV show has a format. These are the key components around which your presentation is based. When I worked on the radio, the formats were very finely timed. For many years as a breakfast show presenter, I followed my show format slavishly, to the minute, every day arriving neatly in time for the GMT pips at seven o'clock and eight o'clock. That didn't happen through coincidence, it was a consequence of careful timing and formatting.

On a podcast, you don't have the same relentless time constraints of radio, it's up to you how you organise the format. However, it's worth bearing in mind the key principles of show formats to keep your show consistent, with direction and impetus. Your format is part of your branding, it's what listeners come to expect from you. It also prevents your show from being directionless, creating anchor points and predictability.

When we devised radio show formats, we would start with the fixed points. On my shows, the news was on the hour and on the half-hour. Weather and sport followed the news on the half-hour. Travel bulletins came before the news on the half-hour and on the hour and lasted one - two minutes. I had to leave sufficient time for the travel update up to the hour so that I could tease the next hour of the show and hit the GMT pips on time. Once you put those anchor points in place, you can see that much of your show is already taken care of. All you have to do is to insert the bits in between.

Some presenters used to devise their format around a pie chart, dividing each hour up into five-minute segments. I always preferred a linear plan on a sheet of A4, with the timings written on the left-hand side of the page. However, it's the concept that's important here; you need to think about the format of your show, and it doesn't need to be a complicated one.

Here's my format for my weekly self-publishing diaries. There's no rocket science involved, but it creates the structure around which each show is based:

Title: Paul's Podcast Diary - Episode [*Episode number goes here*]

Date: [*Date goes here*]

Coming up this week:

1 - [*Headline 1 goes here*]
2 - [*Headline 2 goes here*]
3 - [*Headline 3 goes here*]

This week's writing word count …

> [Details here]

This week's editing update …

> [Details here]

My general writing news …

> [*Item 1 goes here*]
> [*Item 2 goes here*]
> [*Item 3 goes here*]

This week's listener mentions …

> [Details here]

Outro …

I'll have another diary update for you next Saturday – in the meantime have a great week of writing!

How simple is that? It's useful because it allows me to jot down notes and thoughts as each week passes. By the time I get to Friday – diary recording day – I've already got my show planned and it doesn't take me any time to do it. The format also creates a framework for my show notes, but more on that later.

Here's the format I used for my crypto podcast, not a lot changes, but we used two presenters on that show, so you can see how I indicated who was speaking and when:

Episode XX: [INSERT SHOW TITLE]

Presenter 1: Welcome to the Crypto News Podcast Episode number XX for Saturday XX YY ZZ ... this episode is called [INSERT SHOW TITLE]

Presenter 2: Coming up in today's show:

Teaser 1
Teaser 2
Teaser 2

Presenter 1 leads - alternate stories: Top 5 Crypto News Stories from The Past Seven Days

5 > Headline + Text + article URL

4 > Headline + Text + article URL

3 > Headline + Text + article URL

2 > Headline + Text + article URL

1 > Headline + Text + article URL

This week's top story > Headline + Text + article URL

Presenter 2: This Week's Crypto Portfolio Performance:

[Portfolio value + Top crypto + Worst crypto]

Presenter 1 leads - alternate stories: This Week's Crypto Quickies

1 > Story summary + article URL

2 > Story summary + article URL

3 > Story summary + article URL

Presenter 2: Outro - That's it for another week on The Crypto News podcast.

Presenter 1: We'll be back next Saturday with more crypto news, tips and gossip.

Bye for now!

I recommend scripting your intro and outro, and busking around notes for the rest of the show.

It's important that your podcast has a strong beginning because many people will make a judgement about its content based entirely on that small sampler. They'll click on that little audio icon, listen to the introduction, get a feel for your voice, professionalism and content, and very quickly decide whether to continue based on that small amount of research. If you sound like your show is a mess, or you haven't got a clue what's going on, they're unlikely to continue listening.

I need to add a dash of caution to this advice. Do not – under any circumstances – script your entire show. Do not let your guests script their interview responses. It will sound terrible, it always does. One of the skills of being a radio presenter is seamlessly gliding between a script and ad-libbing. Scripted shows sound terrible - work from bullet points. I'm going to say more about this later on in the book when I pass on lots of practical presentation tips to you, but for now, a reiteration: do not script your entire show, ever.

I'm a fan of teasers after working for so many years in radio. Everybody's competing for your ears in podcast land, so it's essential that you give listeners compelling reasons to keep listening. You'll hear radio presenters doing it all the time, whether they're promising you the chance to win a big prize, tempting you with a celebrity interview, previewing a breaking news story or promising to play a classic music track. All of this is designed to stop you switching over to another channel.

The trick of writing great teasers is to think like a newspaper headline writer. Don't give away the full story, just tell enough of it to make it irresistible; the listener has to know what it's about. Use phrases like:

- I'll reveal the true story/facts/hidden story behind XYZ
- I'll tell you what happened when I did XYZ this week
- It's been a week of disasters; we'll tell you what went wrong ...
- We'll have the results of XYZ

- I'll be asking you the most important question there is about XYZ

Nothing is revealed in those headlines, but given that the listener is interested in my podcast topic in the first place, they're going to find it hard to resist content that is framed like this.

The intro and outro are also part of your show's format. This is a good time to use a catchphrase or identifying words to establish your podcast brand and set out your stall.

You might begin with: *Hello, welcome to the XYZ podcast, the weekly show for teenage musicians who are hell-bent on having a hit single before they turn 30.* That's strong, clear and distinctive branding and it gives a confident start to each episode, signposting clearly what the listener is in for.

At the end of my self-publishing podcast, I say a simple *Have a great week of writing!* It's not fussy, it relates to my topic and it signals the end of my show. You don't need to make life difficult for yourself; don't overcomplicate things, these are simply signposting for your show.

Have you ever been talking to somebody in an office and they stand up at their desk, signalling that as far as they're concerned, it's the end of the conversation? These signposts work the same way in your podcast. When your listeners hear you saying certain things they'll think 'Oh, I like this bit!' or 'Oh dear, that's the show over for this week!' These are markers and road signs which effectively navigate listeners through your episodes.

As with all the things I'm telling you, if you're a massive celebrity who already has a rapid following, frankly you can do as you please. Your listeners have bonded with you already, they'd turn up to support you if you were blowing up balloons in a dog's kennel. For the rest of us, these techniques work.

Podcast presenters

Will you be a Lone Ranger, or will your podcast feel like a party? These things matter because they create a different show dynamic. I've presented radio shows on my own and I've worked on double-headed shows, which is just a radio way of saying that I co-presented. In actual fact, even if I anchored a radio show, I always had co-presenters taking care of news, weather, sport and travel.

I'll be honest with you, it's a lot easier presenting on your own; you only have yourself to please and you don't have to make sure two of you aren't speaking at the same time. However, I've had a lot of laughs co-presenting, even though it makes the logistics more complicated. I've had to co-present on the radio with people that I loved working with and others who I didn't particularly care for. I'm sure some of my co-presenters didn't much care for me at times too. I once asked a co-presenter if she had ever shorn a sheep and she was horrified at the suggestion. At the time, I'd shorn sheep on three separate occasions in my radio presenting career, so it seemed to be a reasonable question to ask. On the radio you just get on with it and make it sound like everybody you speak to is your best mate.

When you set up your own podcast, it's up to you who you present with. You get to choose. For my weekly self-publishing podcast, I present alone and bring in guests who I want to chat to. I intentionally co-presented the crypto show with a writing colleague who was an excellent choice, even if I do say so myself. The trick with finding a great co-presenter is in making sure you're sufficiently different to create some contrast, but not so different that there's no spark or chemistry there. You need to get on well and find someone who you can chat to easily. But also, they have to be reliable. Refer back to all the things I've asked you: is your co-presenter as committed as you are? If they're not, it won't be long until you're left high and dry and on your own.

Think of it like a marriage; granted, you won't be leaving the top off the toothpaste or placing the toilet seat in an unacceptable position. However, you are going to be living your relationship out in the open, in front of an audience, and you need to get on with each other.

Of course, solo and double-headed aren't the only formats you can use. Here are some others:

- Zoo format (several people, with a party atmosphere).
- Rotating presenters (useful if somebody can't commit every week).
- Guest presenters (you anchor the show, invite a special guest to co-host from time to time).
- Stand-in presenter (when you go away on your holidays, a recognised, but occasional presenter).

The world is your oyster when it comes to presentation formats. But let me repeat this just for the record: it's more fun with other people, but the more moving parts your podcast has, the less likely it is that you'll be able to sustain it without interruption.

Podcast frequency

How often will you release your podcast? Weekly? Bi-weekly? Monthly? Daily? If you answered *annually* it may be time to make some different life choices.

The final decision is yours, but let me be really strict here. Pick a podcast frequency and stick to it; don't mess around. If you're nervous about your ability to sustain your show, just make it a monthly episode. As you gain in confidence and your processing speed improves, you may wish to announce that you're moving to a bi-weekly format. It's entirely up to you, but I'd recommend not biting off more than you can chew at first.

I started by recording weekly guest interviews and that pace was relentless as I did everything on my own and was still at work at the time. I maintained it for a couple of years, but made it monthly in the end, then seasonal, which I'll explain in more detail later on.

What you absolutely mustn't do is to release episodes whenever you feel like it. That really doesn't work for the majority of listeners, they need to be able to rely on you and set their clocks by your release schedule. Give yourself the best chance of having a podcast which lasts the course. Be realistic about the amount of time you have at your disposal and pick a release schedule accordingly.

A final word about podcast seasons, and for this, I have to credit Colin Gray, UK podcast supremo who I'll be saying more nice things about towards the end of this book. This idea is inspired, and I wish I'd heard Colin share this tip before I started podcasting. You don't have to podcast every week, forever. A really clever way of getting started is to plan and release your show in seasons. This sets you up for success from the outset.

By way of example, season one of my podcast might have been titled *How to plan a new podcast*, and sketched out over ten episodes as follows:

Week 1: Choosing your audience
Week 2: Selecting your topic
Week 3: Checking out the competition
Week 4: Coming up with a title
Week 5: Devising a show format
Week 6: Presentation options
Week 7: How often will you release episodes?
Week 8: Evergreen or news format?
Week 9: What to talk about
Week 10: Putting it all together + season 2 preview

I could release those episodes at the rate of one per week, for ten weeks, then take a month off in between seasons in order to give myself a break. In fact, so long as you're clear with your audience when the next season begins – and you stick to that date – you could leave a gap of three months if you really wanted to. Seasons are the super-power every podcast host needs to enable them to keep their show going in the long term and I commend it to you as a release strategy and an attractive alternative to just putting out episodes forever, until you either give up, retire or die of old age.

A legal word in your ear

This is just a brief warning, in order to set out my stall before you dive too deep in. I'll expand this later in the book, but I want to flag up from a very early stage that as a podcast host you have the same legal obligations as the BBC when it comes to things like libel, copyright and contempt of court. Seriously, you can't just wash your hands of responsibility, when you start a podcast; you are a broadcaster and the same rules apply.

Social media is the same. You may have seen legal cases around things people have said – or shared – on social media which have landed them in serious legal trouble. When you post on social media, the same rules apply as they would to a newspaper or other media outlet. You can't say whatever you want to say (though to be fair, you can still say a lot): you can't help yourself to the latest tune from Coldplay for your intro music, you can't play in clips from films for your weekly reviews, and you can't make terrible allegations about that guy at work who you don't like.

Consider this an early warning. I'll go into more detail later, but I'm raising it now because you may have opted for a podcast topic which includes something that I mentioned above. As a consequence, you could be heading for choppy waters.

I don't want to scare you off either. I've broadcast hundreds, maybe thousands, of hours of audio content and never had a legal issue, not even on live phone-in radio which can be a potential minefield of legal nightmares. Later in the book, I'll give you some simple rules to follow which will help to keep you out of trouble. Fortunately, I got trained in this stuff before they let me anywhere near a live microphone.

Key points

- There are many decisions to make before starting your podcast. Think about your niche, whether your show will be timeless or topical, your SEO-friendly title, show format and frequency and your preferred configuration of presenters.

- Podcasting takes persistence and tenacity – it's best to start with ten episodes in the first instance to see how you like it.
- Listen to other podcasts in your niche to get a feel for their content and style.

4

PODCASTING EQUIPMENT

I'm going to set out my stall early when it comes to podcasting equipment. I do not subscribe to the *buy-loads-of-equipment-at-great-expense* school of philosophy. This is a perilous route and I advise you to avoid it.

Many podcast gurus will overwhelm you with expensive equipment choices which will make your credit card wince. You are not going to get any nonsense like that in this book. If that's what you're looking for, I'm not going to give it to you. Instead, my advice is this: **keep it simple.**

There's a great phrase which is used for people who take up a new hobby, buy all the gear – the goggles, the figure-hugging trousers, the fluorescent tops, the outrageously expensive trainers – and then look, frankly, ridiculous. *All the gear and no idea* – doesn't that just say it all? Don't be that type of podcaster. Start with simple, affordable equipment and – if and when your podcast takes off and advertisers are beating a path to your door – then, and only then, can you ramp it up, invest in the recording studio previously used by Deep Purple, Genesis and the like, and go mega professional. In the meantime, be happy being able to broadcast to listeners all over the world from your kitchen table using just a laptop and some very simple kit.

Microphone overview

You can spend a fortune on microphones. Seriously, you could spend hundreds of pounds if you wanted to. Please don't even think about it. I'm going to give you a simple rule of microphones. It doesn't matter how much it costs, how cool it looks, whether you bought it new or second-hand. Get ready for my profound and highly technical test ... are you ready?

How does it sound when you record with it?

That's it. Can we hear your voice properly? Is it a tinny, muffled mess or are we reading you loud and clear? If you're using a tin can attached to a piece of string, I'll hazard a guess that won't pass my test. If you're using a microphone that costs over £20 and plugs into a USB socket on your laptop, it'll probably be fine to get you started.

Let's also talk about technical matters. This is a labyrinth of hell if you get caught up in it. When I was on the radio, I used to turn up, open my mouth and let the engineers take care of all the technical stuff. I didn't care if it was directional, non-directional or omnidirectional, dynamic, condenser, lapel, shotgun, what the frequency response was, the sensitivity, whether it had phantom power or what the maximum SPL number was. That way lies madness. None of it even matters if you never release your first episode – remember, *all the gear and no idea*?

Here are some realities of podcasting. Most people who listen to you will care more about *what* you say rather than the frequency response of your microphone – unless, of course, it's a podcast about microphones. You could have the best microphone in the history of all microphones; if what's coming out your mouth is boring and irrelevant, it won't improve your content. Let's focus on the stuff that matters and ditch the stuff that doesn't.

In addition, when I listen to podcasts, I'm usually running, driving or walking and I'm surrounded by ambient sound. The audio will probably be mixed down to mono as it's voice only and the file size will be small enough so that many episodes can be downloaded to a phone without using up all the available storage space. This is not radio! If we were engineering a classical concert with a full orchestra which was being broadcast in stereo via FM radio, now *that's* a professional engineering job and one which requires high levels of expertise and experience. But your first podcast? Not so much.

With all that said, I am going to give you some guidance in this area, so that you're not stumbling in the dark. Just remember, the quality of what comes out of your mouth – your show's content – will not be impacted in any way by how much you spend on equipment. Let's keep it simple, let's get your podcast launched and on its way, then we can get all fancy-pants with the kit if and when the money is rolling in.

Microphone & headphone sets

My self-publishing podcast involved me interviewing new authors in its early days and many of my guests had never even appeared on a podcast before. To allow for this, I created a briefing page for guests (more on this technique later) in which I offered the following advice:

Do I need to worry about any technical matters?

It will help if you have an external microphone, rather than one that is built-in, to ensure that the recording quality is good enough.

Want to be a 'Pro' podcast guest?

If you'd like to be a guest on other podcasts, as well as mine, here's a tip! Always have a decent microphone and always use headphones. You owe it to yourself (and the podcast host) to make sure that the audio quality is as good as possible. Here is my recommendation for the cheapest, most basic level of microphone & headphone combo if it's time to invest in a bit of decent equipment. There's much better available, of course, but this will make sure that you're sounding good when the interview is recorded.

Logitech H390 USB Headset

This headset is very reasonably priced. It plugs into a USB socket on your desktop computer or laptop and comes with no technical hassles. I'm pretty sure I have Dave Jackson from The School of Podcasting to thank for that recommendation and yes, I own one myself. By the way, I will be recommending Dave Jackson as a great source of further information at the end of this book. Dave gives great advice. He tests and reviews super-cool microphones, but his recommendations are always sensible and practical. Like me, he'll tell you not to overstretch your budget at the start. But if and when you are ready to get more ambitious with your rig, I recommend checking out Dave's podcast for informed and measured guidance.

I'm going to stick my neck out here and tell you that a Logitech headset is all you need to get started. It sounds absolutely fine, it's suitable for most budgets and if you follow the guidance in this book, you can get away with making that your only purchase before you launch your podcast. I'm telling you how to launch a podcast for under £40 here – a show which, in time, could potentially be worth a fortune. Don't worry, you can thank me later. I'll tell you where to send the cheques to at the end of the book.

If you have a USB headset already – it doesn't have to be that particular model, it's just my recommendation if you have to buy new – that will probably be fine too, you don't need to replace it. Just apply my simple, highly technical test: *How does it sound when you record with it?* Another point I'll raise at this stage is that microphone technique is also an important factor in how you sound. This relates to the positioning of the microphone and how you regulate your voice, and also the level of ambient sound. I'll be covering these topics in more detail later in the book, but once again, this will help to reassure you that you have many more basic considerations to take care of before you remortgage your house to buy a costly podcasting kit.

Microphones

At this stage, I'm going to admit to you that I don't use a Logitech headset to record my own podcasts. Before I even left the BBC, I did my research and splashed out over £100 on my trusty and faithful Audio Technica microphone. At the time of writing, these microphones are still available. The microphone came with a small and simple mounting tripod and a USB connection lead.

At that time, I was seeking a microphone that would

replicate as accurately as possible the lovely, rich sound that I got when I broadcast on FM on a BBC radio show. And that was my first disappointment. I was unable to recreate that sound. The reason for that was not just due to the microphone.

I was recording in my small study; you could hear ambient noise outside (that darn wood pigeon, the occasional siren, and every now and then, the dreaded lawn cutter), and my chair squeaked every time I shuffled. The simple truth is that although you might get close to it, you'll never achieve that wonderful sound unless you're actually recording in a broadcast-equipped studio. By the way, you can hire studios like this to record your podcast if you want to. They cost a lot of money, they'll burn up your budget and I'll remind you once again of what's more important than all of this – what comes out of your mouth. If that's rubbish and nonsense, none of that expense will make any difference.

I'm going to admit something else to you now; I haven't a clue about microphones. If I decided to go all fancy-pants with my podcasting, I'd book a 15-minute consultation with Dave Jackson from The School of Podcasting (can you see a theme developing here?). Dave's been around the block several times with podcasting. If you tell him your budget, advise him on your set-up (i.e. single voice, dual presenter etc), he'll steer you right. I'd like you to use that cheap Logitech to get started because I want you to succeed as a podcaster. I want to show you a simple route to success and fast results so that you get caught by the podcasting bug. Once you're caught by the bug and generating an income through your show, you have my permission to get as fancy as you want to.

Many people choose Yeti microphones, and you'll see these are widely recommended if you do any reading around. I bought a Yeti once, thinking I was missing out, and I didn't get on with it. Firstly, it was heavy. As a former radio presenter, I prefer to have my microphone on a boom arm (I'll explain more shortly) so that I can move it exactly where I want it. Old habits die hard. The Yeti has four pickup patterns – cardioid, omni, bidirectional and stereo pickup – and already we're getting too complicated if you're a podcast newbie. I found that it picked up every hand movement on my desk and was like positioning a brick to speak into. I sent it back and fortunately, I got a refund. Don't take my word for it though. Most microphones have YouTube reviews – my AT2020 did – so check them out and see what people are saying about them. At the time I'm typing this, my AT2020 remains undefeated and has cost me about £10 for each year of use. I'd say that worked out pretty well for a purchase.

It's worth mentioning that I have, reluctantly, recorded with some guests who have ignored my advice about buying a basic microphone. I can tell you that Apple built-in microphones are generally quite impressive and even non-Apple built-in microphones have given me acceptable audio in the past. However, as the host of the show, it's crucial that your audio is as good as we can get it within your budget, so please give serious consideration to using something basic, at least.

In summary, when it comes to selecting your microphone, please do not get lost in the wilderness of tech, 'hi-fi experts', expensive gadgetry or 'the latest thing'. Start simple, as I advise, get your first ten podcast episodes in the pot, see how you feel about podcasting, and ramp things up if your budget – and your enthusiasm – allow.

Windshields

I talked a short time ago about the importance of microphone technique. This relates to your use of the microphone, and with all things in life, there's a right way and a wrong way. If you speak too loudly you will 'over-mod' as we used to call it in radio: over-modulate. That means your voice will be distorted when you listen back to it and there will be very little you can do to put it right afterwards. A good rule of thumb with recording audio is *rubbish in-rubbish out*. Although modern software gives you many more options than I had when I started my career recording interviews on ¼ inch tape, it can't work miracles.

The primary purpose of a windshield is to eliminate what's known as 'mic popping' in the trade. This term refers to that *pop* sound you get when somebody says a word beginning with the letter *p*. Try saying a couple of words that begin with that letter and note what your breath does. It sends an air bullet directly at the microphone and this can result in a nasty effect on your recording. It often means that your microphone technique needs to be adjusted – move a little further away from the microphone – but it also indicates that a windshield would make sense for you.

My AT2020 microphone is very susceptible to mic popping and I would not use it for voice recording without a microphone windshield attached to it. These windshields cost very little and I'd generally advise you to use one at all times unless you're using a combined microphone and headset, many of which are designed to reduce that problem anyway, due to the close proximity of the microphone to the mouth.

A word of warning though; windshields attach to microphones in different ways, so make sure that you're buying the correct shield for your unit. Mine clips on, others are attached by spring-loaded contraptions, some are rounded foam covers. Foam windshields perform the same job and may just slide over the end of your microphone. My best tip is to look on a retailer like Amazon and see the *Frequently Bought Together* options which often indicate the correct bit of kit to use. Once again, you don't need to spend a fortune, keep it cheap and simple, but you will find that combining this item with a microphone will spare you many editing headaches in your podcasting future.

Microphone stands

My AT2020 came supplied with a simple tripod which had an attachment to securely hold the microphone. This is fine for most purposes, but I used my microphone to record training videos for several years before I even started podcasting. I used to find the positioning inconvenient – directly in front of me – because it got in the way when I was working from a desktop computer screen. I tend to read my show notes from my desktop computer screen too, so the tripod never worked for me. However, a corporate podcast that I advised on also used an AT2020 and the tripod works fine for them because it's only used for a two-person interview format.

I also find that stands which sit on a desk can sometimes mean that the microphone picks up taps, hand movements and pen sounds if you're writing notes as you go along. You can mitigate this by placing the stand on a rubber mat; a simple, cheap mouse mat from your local pound store will suffice.

Microphone stands are simple, cheap and portable; don't over-egg the pudding if you don't need to.

Microphone arms

As a radio presenter, my microphones were always mounted on an adjustable arm, much like an anglepoise lamp arm. This allows the user to position the microphone exactly where it's wanted. You can sit or stand when using it and move it out of the way if you need to access your keyboard for any reason. It's my preferred way of working, but please remember, I worked for nearly two decades in radio studios before I started this podcasting lark; it's definitely not a 'must-have'. If you take a look on Amazon, you'll see that you can buy these adjustable stands – along with custom windshields – for less than £20.

A word of warning though; these arms use a small vice-like mechanism to attach to your desk. Depending on where you'll be recording your podcast, a simple tripod might be less of a problem and much more portable. I'd only recommend a movable arm like this if you record in the same place most of the time and it can remain attached to your desk on an ongoing basis.

Headphones

You're only going to need headphones if you interview guests who are not sitting directly opposite you. You may also need them if you record through a mixing desk, but that's more advanced than I intend to tackle in this book.

When you see presenters portrayed on the television wearing headphones, I think it somehow creates the impression that you can't record a podcast without them. Let me explain why headphones are used in a radio studio, so we can put that one to bed.

In a radio studio, I would monitor the FM output to

make certain my show was making it to the transmitters and beyond. You might think that I'd have to monitor what was coming out of the studio, which I was also able to do with the flick of a switch. But we would monitor the radio station output as the listener heard it; it was also the first clue for me that something had gone wrong technically.

I was once presenting a radio show on a Friday evening and somebody – who shall remain nameless, but who should have known better – was messing around with buttons in the main technical area. Reader, he took me off air. As a presenter, the first warning I got was that my headphones went silent; I knew we had gone off air. When that happens, if the engineers aren't aware already, you holler for help. But here's where the headphones come in again, I'm running blind if I can't hear my guests, audio reports and CDs. I immediately switched to local output i.e. what I was sending to the transmitter, rather than what the transmitter is sending out. I monitored like that until I got the nod that we were back on air. Just because you go off air, you don't stop broadcasting and go home. You carry on as if nothing has happened until you get the nod from engineering that the problem is fixed. Then you switch that button back to FM output and continue monitoring all over again.

By the way, we went off air three times that I can recall in my broadcasting career. The first time it happened was the first time I ever went on-air live with a BBC show. Of course, the obvious conclusion was that I'd messed something up; even I thought that. Turns out I hadn't – the engineers had been working on something and hadn't put it back properly.

So how does that apply to podcasting? Well, it means you only need to use headphones if you're recording a voice call over the internet via Skype or Zoom (more on them later) to avoid feedback. Feedback is an awful echoing sound caused by audio going round and round through a microphone and headphones or speaker in a cycle of audio Armageddon. If you have a more ambitious rig with a mixing desk, you'll want somebody monitoring what's actually getting picked up by the microphones, in which case you will need headphones in this scenario too.

I'll deal with the former later in this book as it pertains to the simple set-ups which this book is focusing on. I'm not the guy to talk to you about mixing desks and fancy rigs, they're outside the scope of what I'm doing here. As a broadcaster, I'd turn up and it was all neatly set out for me. There's a lesson in that; you're a broadcaster, not an engineer. Spend as much time as possible on the jobs which involve broadcasting; avoid the technical distractions that are the work of an engineer. Unless, of course, it's an engineer you want to be rather than a podcaster.

Phone apps

Brace yourself for a *when I was a boy* story!

When I was a cub reporter, I recorded onto a reel of ¼ inch tape on a Uher recording device which was heavier than a packed rucksack. If it started losing charge, I'd have to encourage it by winding the plastic tape reels with a pencil. If I was recording long interviews, I'd have to change tapes halfway through the conversation. And that's not the worst of it. Sometimes you'd get electrical sounds or terrible 'mic rattle', where a succession of rushing reporters had abused the cables that ran from the microphone to the Uher connector, or if your cable was swinging about and tapping something nearby. Kids today don't know how easy they have it.

These days I have a phone app on my Android phone.

Old habits die hard, but if ever I was on the scene of a breaking news story, I'd grab my phone, open up my app, record that audio interview and send it to my local radio station. My chosen app is called Hi-Q. It comes as a free download, but I have upgraded it to lose the adverts and any restrictions. Apps like this are two a penny and the built-in microphones on phones are pretty good these days. If you still use an old-fashioned Nokia phone, that doesn't apply to you. And if you're an iPhone user, there's a built-in and free Voice Memos app available to you.

So why am I telling you this? Well, recently I recorded a podcast episode on the beach at Benidorm, the sound of the sea in the background. Sometimes you can use 'atmos' to great effect – that's short for atmosphere by the way – though make sure it isn't so loud that it's hard to make out your voice, and always avoid music in the background, not only for copyright reasons (more on that later!), but also because it's a devil to edit. I've spent years as a reporter – and now as a podcaster – asking hotels and pubs to switch off the background music. Believe me, you make the mistake of having music in the background once in your career, then you vow to never let it happen again.

I have also made at least four podcast recordings on location, at conferences or in the interviewee's place of work. It's handy to have an app available, just in case you ever need it. Most professions host conferences or exhibitions and I'll bet you attend some of these. They're a great place to gather audio for your podcast, so do have a simple recording app on your phone just in case you ever spot an opportune moment to record with someone.

Handheld recorders

You do not need a handheld recorder, but depending on how much on-location podcast recording you end up doing, you may decide to invest in something that's a little more robust and flexible than your phone. I'm really not snobby about phones, they do a great job, but I did decide to splash out and get a bit of kit that was specifically built for the job.

Once again, a word of warning. You do not need one of these devices to become a podcaster, nor do you need to spend a lot of money on one. The primary reason for me buying one was to ensure that I always had sufficient recording time available to me (a phone's storage can fill very quickly) and that I could attach a simple tripod so that I didn't get vibrations or tapping noises from a phone that I was either holding or that was sitting on a table.

I purchased a Tascam device for about £100. If you do go down this path, I'd personally recommend a Tascam or a Zoom device. When you're searching on Amazon look for a handheld audio recorder and take care not to buy a digital recorder, which tends to be set up for dictation rather than interviewing. You may need to consider the additional purchase of a windshield too. Finally, check that your device incorporates a tripod mount, this will enable you to attach my preferred type of tripod for portable use: a Joby or 'octopus' style holder. You could, of course, just use your phone and get a bespoke tripod for that.

Only buy this kit if and when you're going to use it, buy within your personal budget and remember that a smartphone plus free app does the job just as well.

Soundproofing

I'll tackle this topic in a little more detail later in the book, but there's no point having the most expensive microphone in the world if you're broadcasting from a toilet. That means you need to give some consideration to your surroundings. I have laminate flooring in my study, so before I moved in my desk and shelves, I fitted some cheap carpet – it was an off-cut – in order to make the recorded sound warmer.

I also did something that's a little excessive; I measured my window and purchased some specially-cut audio foam (priced at about £60) which fits into the window frame recess whenever I'm recording something special. It makes the room sound less empty. Before I started podcasting, I used to record online training videos. Over the course of a day, there would be all sorts of extraneous sounds from beyond my window, and I was keen to shut them out. My audio foam helped me to do just that. Do I use it when I record my podcast episodes? No, I don't. To be honest, it doesn't make that much difference. However, I've mentioned it here in case it proves useful to you if you find that your recording environment sounds like a public lavatory.

Sound shields

Sound shields must have been available when I first set out to record at home via my computer, but I wasn't aware of them back then or else I would have purchased one. These are priced at about £80 – Marantz produces a nice, sturdy one – and they help to create a warmer, less hollow sound when recording in a large room or a room without carpets. Essentially, they create a small audio booth which will sit on your kitchen table, the interior of which is lined with a specially-designed audio foam which stops your voice getting lost in the room. Some people even line cardboard boxes with foam or thick fabric and place their microphone inside; improvise if you have to, this is audio only, nobody can see you.

With the corporate podcast I helped to set up, interviews are most often recorded in the boardroom, a large area which is very comfortable, but not best suited as a recording environment. We purchased a Marantz sound shield to help us to tame the natural environment and it works a treat.

You might get lucky and find that the place where you record your podcast episodes is fine from the get-go. However, if it is less than ideal, the cavalry is always close at hand and a practical solution nearby.

Mixers

Hopefully, by now, you can already anticipate what I'm going to say about mixers; you don't need one. The most frequent podcasting scenario where you're going to need to think about it is if there are two or more of you recording in the same room, each using a separate microphone. Now, once again, there's no reason why you can't just huddle around a single microphone while you're starting out, it'll certainly help you get to know your co-presenter well.

In the corporate podcast that I mentioned earlier, the presenter and guest sit either side of the corner of that long table in the boardroom, so they can face each other and speak across the microphone which is positioned dead centre and facing towards both of them. The sound shield is positioned behind the tripod-mounted microphone and it works just fine.

I'm not going to get embroiled with mixing desk discussions in this book, it's not an area of expertise for me, and I'd advise speaking to somebody who can advise properly about these things. My recommended source of further information on this matter is UK podcasting supremo Colin Gray who has great experience in this area. I'll place links to Colin's work at PaulTeague.net/POD.

However, before spending your hard-earned cash on a mixer, please ask yourself if you really need it. I have managed to record over 400 podcasts in all sorts of different environments and I never needed a mixer. Just saying!

Equipment summary

Hopefully, my words of caution are ringing out loud and clear in your ears by now. Having worked with local businesses for many years, I know that people tend to overcomplicate things. If you go down that particular rabbit hole in podcasting, you're likely to end up with a big box full of cables and technical kit under your bed which was taken out of the packaging once and never got used. There's plenty of time to do all this fancy stuff; let's not run before we can walk.

I consider Joanna Penn to be the queen of self-publishing podcasting, as she's been at it for more than a decade now and has built up an amazing catalogue of over 470 episodes. But if you care to listen to Joanna's first episode, it was recorded by placing a microphone next to the mouthpiece of a telephone. Joanna is one of the most respected voices in the self-publishing arena, people fly her all over the world to hear her speak. She started her podcast simply, with the equipment that was available to her at the time. The reason that her podcast flourished is that the content is superb and thousands of people all over the world download it every week, me included. There's always plenty of time to improve and make things better. Your first priority is to get started and get your podcast out there in the first place.

You will always be judged most on your content. Sure, your audio must be of a certain standard which is easily attained following the advice in this chapter. But never let your technical equipment get you so tied up in knots that you don't ever get as far as releasing that first episode.

Key points

- Keep it simple when it comes to equipment. There's plenty of time to spend money on better kit when your show is established.
- A Logitech H390 USB Headset is a great place to start if you're on a limited budget.
- Windshields, microphone stands, boom arms and sound shields might also be useful depending on where you record your podcast.

5

LAUNCHING YOUR PODCAST

There are two key components in creating a podcast. You have to record your show, then you need to upload it somewhere so that it can be syndicated, and other people can download it. Sounds simple, doesn't it?

This can be a bit of a minefield without somebody to guide you through it, as there are a number of different services and delivery techniques available and you could waste a month trying to figure out which to go for. As with everything in this book, I've gone through the pain so that you don't have to. What I've outlined below is the way I do things, but I've been mindful of a number of factors in making my recommendations.

I'll focus firstly on how we're going to distribute your new podcast. The reason I've gone for this option to get started is that I'm going to steer you in the way of a free service first of all which will let you record and syndicate your show using a single tool. Basically, it does everything, and it won't cost you a thing. You won't even have to sell your soul to use it.

Let's get tucked into the practical stuff now. Ready to get your hands dirty? Here we go!

Podcast hosting

There are many ways to host a podcast. When I started out, I bought a software service which allowed me to record and process my shows, then upload them and distribute them. Guess what? The people who created it stopped maintaining it, so it became all but useless very quickly. Fingers burned, lesson learned. Why am I telling you this? Because you need to select a service which has been around for a while, and which looks like it'll be hanging around for a while longer. It's a pain having to transfer over an existing podcast to an alternative service. I recommend you avoid it at all costs, unless you're growing fast, getting lots of downloads and it's a position forced upon you by excellent growth.

So why do you need podcast hosting? I'll keep this as geek-free as possible, I promise. When you record your podcast, it will most likely be a .mp3, .wav or – if you're super-cool – an M4A file. Once recorded, you will be able to play that file on your desktop computer, but nobody else will be able to access it. We have to syndicate it in some way and place it on a server where *everybody* with the link can access it. Now, if you wanted to, you could upload the audio file to your own website, if you have one. Before long you'd receive warnings from your web host telling you that you've burned through your monthly bandwidth allowance and your site has been taken down until your new allocation kicks in next month. Here's a tip: *never* host audio or video on your own server, unless you're rich or called Jeff Bezos. It's an expensive business and one which you have to be mindful of, just in case your show ever hits the big time.

I heard one of my own podcasting favourites, Joanna Penn, revealing how much she has to pay each month just to deliver the thousands of monthly downloads that she gets on her weekly episodes. It made a grown man cry; it was costing thousands of dollars a year just to deliver her show. Joanna makes her podcast available via Amazon web hosting, a service that I use myself to deliver some of my older training videos and – at first – my own podcast episodes. However, you pay for Amazon web services by usage, and this can escalate very quickly if your show takes off and I'd caution against taking this option. It's also technically quite complicated unless you use a third-party software service to connect it all up. In brief, although you may see this technique suggested elsewhere, I'd give it a wide berth for now. If your podcast takes off and the big bucks start to roll in, you'll always be able to scale up to meet growing audience demands. In the meantime, we'll keep it cheap and simple.

RSS feeds explained

Podcasts are syndicated using a system called RSS, which stands for Really Simple Syndication.

In practical terms, RSS is an easy way to distribute content to a large number of people. It goes back to what I was saying about that audio file sitting on your desktop: how do you get it into as many hands as possible? You use RSS, that's how.

Now, this is background knowledge for you, and you have my permission to forget this bit the moment I tell you about it. However, I don't want you to view your podcast as black magic, it's always good to have a basic understanding of how all this stuff works. In very simple terms, when you podcast, you upload your audio files to somebody else's server and your listeners can access it via an RSS feed, which is like an online subscription. That means each episode is automatically delivered to their phone, desktop computer or laptop. This is the wonderful thing about RSS; once a listener subscribes, it's like having their own personal mail delivery system. Every time you upload a new episode to the server, it gets delivered to them automatically.

This is why podcasts are such a wonderful thing; they're what's known as 'sticky'. Web users don't have to remember to go hunting for your show every week, it gets delivered directly to them, so it makes it much easier to consume your fabulous content. With my internet marketing head on, I call that an efficient marketing machine, working away for you in the background, delivering every new episode like clockwork, so long as you turn up to record it, that is.

Anchor

The quickest, fastest, cheapest way you can get started with podcasting is to use Anchor. It gives you everything you need, removing all technical requirements and holding your hand every step of the way. However, before you get too excited, I will be sounding an important note of caution, because all that glitters is not gold, as the saying goes.

Using Anchor gives you free, no-catches access to the following features:

- hosting and distribution
- integrated recording and editing tools
- podcast analytics
- Apple or Android apps

- a monetisation model (not available in all territories)
- a simple tool to allow listeners to record voice messages then add them to your show
- licence-free music and sound effects

When I see a free service, my antennae immediately start twitching. I begin searching for their monetisation model because if they don't have one, I become concerned about the long-term viability of the company. When you check out Anchor, you'll see that they've been around for a few years and that they're funded by investors. They also have long-term monetisation plans which start with creating a huge podcast marketplace. It's a bit like YouTube for podcasts. If you search for the article titled 'Why You Should Never Pay for Podcast Hosting' by Nir Zicherman, CTO and co-founder of Anchor, you'll be able to check out the long-term plans and ethos of the service. I've made it available at PaulTeague.net/POD to save you hunting for it.

I'm going to make a bold statement here: if you've never set up a podcast or recorded audio before, if this malarkey is completely alien to you, if you hate technology so much it makes your eyes glaze over, then use Anchor and use it for free. It's an excellent service for new and established podcasters, the decision if yours to make if you're happy to use a free service.

Whether you run Anchor via the app on your phone – the app is excellent by the way – or on your desktop computer, it makes the entire process very simple. Follow the tips and techniques in this book to help you plan your show and create great content, and you'll be away in no time. I genuinely believe this is, at the time of writing, the fastest, easiest and best way to quickly and cheaply launch your brand-new podcast project, in spite of my personal reservations over any free service. And if you don't like it? Just move over to another service. We're not knocking down bricks and mortar here; it's the internet, and life is sweet.

By the way, you get a free web page with Anchor, so you don't even have to go through all the hassle of setting up a website.

Libsyn

There's only one other real contender when it comes to podcast hosting and that has to be Libsyn. Now, that doesn't mean there aren't other services out there, it just means this is the one I've used for over four years, it's simple and straightforward, it's never let me down, it's well-respected and has loads of support available. I tried many of the others in my early days. Libsyn is the service I settled on.

If you read widely on podcasting matters, you'll learn about Podbean, Buzzsprout, Spreaker, Audioboom, Blubrry and others. Feel free to try them out, take them for a spin, see how they suit you. They all offer different features, options and pricing models. But if you want to make directly for a robust, reliable and well-priced service, give Libsyn your attention too.

So why do I like it and why have I stuck with it for nearly five years? Five years on the internet is like reaching my golden wedding anniversary; I deserve a gold watch or something like that.

Here's why I like the service, in a nutshell:

- Simple show templates which speed up episode creation.

- Excellent syndication to other services such as Apple, Spotify, Stitcher and Google Podcasts.
- Excellent social options, with automatic posting to Twitter, Facebook and YouTube.
- Great statistics with a view of global podcast reach.
- Ready-made web page for hosting and promoting all podcast episodes.
- Dynamic pricing which allows you to increase or decrease storage space as it's needed.
- Monetisation options, if required.
- Comes with WordPress plugin for easy website integration.
- Ability to schedule episodes and vary release dates.
- Allows you to host and manage multiple podcast shows within a single portal.
- Provides several web player options to allow you – and others – to embed episodes in web pages.
- Reliable and trustworthy, with great support.

As you can tell, I have a lot of time for Libsyn and I have used it quite happily for a long time. Without beating around the bush, if you want to podcast properly and build a quality business around it, you can't go far wrong with Libsyn.

Other podcast hosting services

Although I have never used any other podcasting service, it's worth me noting a selection of the main alternatives. To be honest, I will have considered most of these before setting out on my own podcast journey, but Libsyn was always my first choice in terms of cost and service. I wasn't aware of Anchor at the time I started podcasting, but I would give it a serious look if I was starting out again now.

Please bear in mind my comments below are simple one-liners just to give you a steer on each of the listed services:

Podbean – offers a free option, but it is capped so be aware of that limitation. The basic paid option is a good price and much more future-proof. I like the patron programme option in the more expensive options, that's a great alternative to Patreon.

Buzzsprout – offers a very limited free option for beginners. I'm not keen on the bandwidth restrictions, there's nothing worse than having to monitor storage and bandwidth, it distracts from the creative work.

Spreaker – I considered this option when I was starting out. It has a free starter option and very reasonably priced upgrades. Distribution options are extensive, and the stats measuring is well worth checking out.

Audioboom – There's no free option here, you're straight into paid services. The website is well-designed and simple to understand, all the basic requirements are met by this service.

BluBrry – I came close to using this service mainly because of their Powerpress plugin for WordPress websites; this won't be of any interest to you if you don't use WordPress.

BlogTalkRadio – This is something a little different as it's geared more to a radio-style format, with live broadcasting, call-ins and online conversations. As a former radio presenter, looking at this website gets me all excited at what could be done with this service.

Channels

I mentioned that Libsyn will syndicate your podcast all over the place, and it is worth checking this out whichever service you decide to use. Anchor will send your show to Apple Podcasts, Google Podcasts, Spotify, Stitcher and others. Take a moment to make sure your podcast hosting service is syndicating your show to your preferred channels.

One of the things that Libsyn does, which I really like, is to automatically publish your show to Facebook, Twitter and YouTube. One of the surprises I got as a podcast host is that not everybody listens to your show on their smartphone. I have a small gang of listeners who discovered me, and only listen to me, via YouTube. Libsyn creates a video file out of your audio, with a still image of your logo, so that listeners can access your output online. I've been amazed at how fast those YouTube listens add up.

Libsyn does the same thing with your podcast on Facebook, creating a 'video' version which sits neatly within your Facebook page. Once again, this is how some listeners prefer to consume my content, it's also very socially shareable on this channel.

Finally, Libsyn drops a neat little player into Twitter so that your episodes can be played directly from within the Tweet stream. It's very user-friendly for users of that social channel.

For most podcasts which won't be huge, none of this will change your world, but it will help you to get the word out and grow your audience for free. When I started podcasting, I considered them to be nice-to-haves. Now, with several years of experience behind me, I'm aware of how useful these channels can be when you're desperate to find your audience without having to spend a fortune. When deciding which platform to use, check out the availability of integrated social sharing. Libsyn does a great job of this.

Why not SoundCloud?

Many of you reading this will be aware of SoundCloud and know it to be a widely-used audio service. So why doesn't it get a shout-out in this chapter?

SoundCloud does have a dedicated area for podcasters, and you can even access it free, but it's not really a podcasting host in the true sense. I consider it a great place to make audio tracks available and then to grab their neat-looking embedded players for my website; indeed I use it occasionally for that very purpose. However, where Sound-Cloud falls short is when it comes to syndicating your show to the relevant channels like Apple Podcasts and Google Podcasts. Sure, it creates an RSS feed, but services like Anchor and Libsyn were created just for podcasting, so they do a much better job. SoundCloud is great for hosting audio files, it would be ideal if you were a young band and wanted a place to store and promote your music, but it's not really built for heavy-duty podcasters like me and you.

Key points

- If you want to start your podcast with the

minimum of fuss and technical issues, use Anchor.

- If you want to use a more flexible and popular podcast hosting option, Libsyn is a great bet. There are many other services available, shop around if you want to.
- Your podcast needs an RSS which will allow listeners to subscribe to your show and automatically receive every new episode.

6

PODCAST PRACTICALITIES

It's time to start work on your show. You know how to distribute your episodes to the world; you've thought about your reasons for podcasting and the topic that you'll cover; now it's time to determine what's going to be in your podcast episodes.

I'm a big fan of systems and routines when it comes to podcasts. The sooner you can distil your process, the faster you'll be able to hit your stride. When you're creating a show week after week, it's in your interests to create a 'rinse-and-repeat' formula. The added advantage of this is that if you ever grow to a level where you can hand over tasks to a third party such as a friend, partner, colleague or VA (virtual assistant – I'll cover this in a later chapter), your entire process is recorded and replicable as a series of organised and set steps.

I also believe that routines and systems will give you the best chance of surviving long term. If you approach your show in a haphazard, disorganised way each week, you'll create added stress for yourself.

A well-oiled podcast should be like a sausage factory

(they can be vegetarian or vegan sausages if you prefer) where each episode is a sausage on the conveyor belt and they all arrive, one after the other, well-formed and delicious at the appointed time. Okay, maybe that wasn't the best analogy – but you get my drift, it needs to operate like a production line. If the production line gets interrupted, you'll start to create stress and panic for yourself and before you know it, you'll be thinking about reducing that stress by removing the root cause of it i.e. the podcast.

Let me share how I do it, using best practice from my years in radio, but adapting these techniques for the modern medium of podcasting.

Show formats

It's crucial to have a show format. I showed you how to do this earlier in the book. If you've forgotten already, move back to Go, do not collect £200. Sorry, that's Monopoly, but you get the gist. You need to know about this stuff. Listeners like formats. Features within your show act as triggers. The listener will think 'I like this bit' or 'Here comes my favourite bit' and get that dopamine hit equivalent. A format also signposts your show clearly, giving it a sense of predictability and creating a rhythm.

People forge routines around TV and radio; they can do the same with podcasts. My radio alarm switches on at 6.35 am each weekday morning. I like to listen to the newspaper review and that day's review of what happened in the UK parliament, as well as catching the top news story, so I know if the world is about to end and I can bulk-buy bread and water and take to my tin bomb shelter. I get up after the day in parliament review and have my shower.

Later, before work, I listen to a quiz on the local

commercial radio station in the bathroom while I'm cleaning my teeth. I don't stop cleaning my teeth until I've tried to answer all the quiz questions and find out if that day's entrant has won the £500 prize. Once the quiz finishes, it's time to leave the house, or else I'll be late for work.

All over the world people mark their life routines by TV and radio. For years, when I watched the news, we'd go to bed after the late evening bulletin. The credits were our 'time to go to bed' trigger. These days I just read apocalyptic fiction; I find it much more soothing.

The point I'm making is that we're creatures of routine. We like pattern and we like predictability. If the radio quiz is late one morning, I'm late for work. If they miss out on the paper review, I feel cheated. They set up a level of expectation and, as a listener, I expect them to honour that informal contract.

Devising a show format is a basic part of podcasting as far as I'm concerned. It doesn't have to be complicated, but you should give it some thought. This is the skeleton around which each show will hang; it gives your episodes a sense of momentum and progression. Incidentally, it also allows listeners to find switch off points too. If my walk to work lasts ten minutes and the podcast is one hour, I can pause at the end of one feature and pick it up at the beginning of another. Also, a format will help you as the presenter and producer of the show; it will organise and clarify your thoughts as you plan each episode. Devise your format first, everything else will hang off this and be supported by it, like clothing on hangers.

Planning

I would caution against launching into a podcast and just hoping for the best. It's preferable to think it through a bit beforehand. Here is a list of things you might like to think – or panic – about. It's offered in a constructive way because you need to be aware of these potential hurdles:

- What happens if I'm ill?
- What happens when I go on holiday?
- What happens if my co-presenter is ill or goes on holiday?
- What happens if a guest cancels on me?
- What will I do if I'm out of ideas/there's no news one week?
- What happens at Easter, Christmas & New Year?

If you survive beyond the first ten episodes of your podcast and go on to make it to one year, you will encounter most of these problems at least once. The solution to all of them is planning. Always have something tucked up your sleeve, just in case.

I've never missed a show due to illness. There's a Twitter comment somewhere in the ether commending me on my podcast commitment, struggling through a sore throat and obvious discomfort to deliver that week's show. However, I'm really lucky, I enjoy good health (touches wood fast) and so this was the only occasion over a four-year period when I was having some difficulty.

If you are ill, you have several choices. Can you train up a stand-in presenter? If you use a co-presenter, can they anchor the show for you? How about having an 'emergency episode' on standby, just in case? It would need to be timeless, but it could be somebody interviewing you, a list of your top ten tips for your niche or topic, or an episode outlining your favourite resources or sources of information. If you have several episodes out already, it could be a compilation of the best bits, or just a replay of the most popular episode to date. Just have this episode sitting as a draft in Libsyn, Anchor or whatever you use and all you have to do, if you are ill, is to crawl out of your death bed with hot water bottle in hand, blanket wrapped around you, and press the publish button at the appointed time. Then you can crawl back into bed until you've recovered.

If you're really ill, or if a big and serious life event occurs, you'll have to pause the show. I'm not a fan of podcast presenters 'disappearing'; you owe it to your audience to explain that there will be a break in service. You don't have to tell them the details, simply record a very short two-minute audio insert which explains that due to unforeseen circumstances, you have to take a break and that you'll resume episodes as soon as possible. Never leave podcast listeners dangling; you don't have to share intimate details of your life, but you should be clear about what's going on.

Holidays and seasonal breaks – for you or your co-presenter(s) – are a lot more predictable. I once went away to Spain for four weeks over Christmas and New Year and stacked my shows as pre-records while I was absent. If you have a news format which makes that difficult, get creative. Maybe record a guest or two and change the format temporarily while you're away (listeners won't relish the disruption to routine, but it's better than skipping full weeks), use a stand-in presenter, compile a best-of-the-year sequence, record a list of things you've learnt from your previous episodes, ask listeners to send in questions to you while you then go on to read and answer them. I once got my guests to ask me some extra questions at the end of our regular interview, and I compiled my answers into a special episode. I also recorded extra questions with my guests, and these can also be compiled as 'director's cut' content. Think creatively, see what works for you in your niche, but do think it through. The more organised you are, and the less reactive to crises, the more chance you have of survival.

Guests sometimes cancel or re-schedule, it's a pain, but life happens. Occasionally you'll get a no-show. I've had only one no-show in 140 interviews. It was really annoying because this guest reached out to me and I didn't really want to interview him anyway. He just disappeared off the face of the earth. Don't ever be that guy. I'm very strict with interview guests, it's one strike and you're out if you behave like that.

If you run an interview format podcast, record a month, a fortnight or a week ahead. Don't even think about recording the same week an episode goes out unless it's in exceptional circumstances. One month is my recommended lead time on guest recordings. You have to factor several things in such as no-shows, technical issues, editing and processing time. If you're always four guests ahead, you can cope with most eventualities. It might seem like hard work but, believe me, you'll thank me for this advice the first time someone – or something – lets you down. Besides, once you're four episodes ahead, you're still only recording one interview per week, the initial effort is in stacking the first four of those recordings.

Constantly compile a list of prospective guests so that you're ten weeks – yes, I really said ten weeks – ahead of the game. You'll use up guest prospects at a rate of knots in a weekly show; never let that list of prospects dry up, it's the lifeblood of your interview show. Recording interviews is a relentless process. I ran one per week for a couple of years, but that's nothing compared with the incredible John Lee Dumas who releases one episode per day – amazing! By the way, he batch records those interviews in one day, to use his time more efficiently. You should consider doing the same thing, even if you're not recording that many episodes at once, it's a very time-effective way to work.

Finally, what do you do if there's no news in your industry one week? Well, that probably means you picked the wrong niche, or you went too narrow with your topic; this is a good indication that you need to broaden things out. However, I would suggest using some form of collation tool if you run a news-based format. This is how I sustained my cryptocurrency podcast; it means that you have a long list of potential talking points delivered washed and scrubbed to your door like clockwork every week. The simplest, free tool to use is Google Alerts. Set it up for the major keywords in your industry and fix in your preferred update interval. My favourite tool for this job was Feedly, which you can use for free, but which is better if you pay a little for it. Finally, Telegram on your mobile phone has some excellent article collation groups and is well worth checking out.

Great planning will make the podcast process much easier for you. I am on the obsessive side of highly organised, I know that, but I come from a background of having to co-produce and present 15 hours of live radio per week, split up as 5 x 1-hour shows and 5 x 2-hour shows. When I was presenting breakfast shows, I used to co-produce and deliver 22.5 hours of live radio each week. That was split as 5 x 2.5 hours of breakfast show followed, after a breakfast break, by 5 x 2 hours of phone-in. I loved every minute of it I hasten to add, but what got us there, every show, day in, day out, week in, week out? Planning and show formats, that's what. There's a reason why TV and radio shows operate like this; it works.

Intros & outros

I've already talked about the importance of intros and outros, but it's time to dig a little deeper now. We need to get these tied down before you launch your show. In short, what will you do about this? Here are some options:

- You read the intro and outro 'live' every week as part of your notes.
- You record your intro and outro in your voice in a voice-only format and use the same recording each week.
- You record your intro and outro and mix with music and use the same recording each week.
- You get somebody else to record your intro and outro and mix with music and use the same recording each week.
- You use the same theme music every week, with no voice-over element.

If you're completely new to this game and have never edited audio before, I'm going to recommend that you pass on options 3, 4 & 5 for now. Option 4 will require outsourcing, which can be done very cheaply, but requires you mixing music and voice in an edit. This can be done very badly; it's the thing I used to coach young journalists about most frequently in my management days with the BBC. It's horrible if you get a voice and music mix wrong; it's best done with a bit of support or paying somebody who knows what they're doing to sort it out. However, if you're fixed on these options, make sure you read about outsourcing later in the book and please, please, please, however boring it sounds, read what I say later about music copyright. You can't just help yourself to your favourite pop tune and use it on your podcast. You'll likely end up in court if you do that. Copyright rules apply here, and you need to take great care when selecting music for your show; more on that later. By the way, Anchor can help here, it makes licence-free music available to you as part of the free service.

This leaves us with options 1 & 2, by far my preferred choices for podcast newbies. Option 1 is the easiest and the format I'm going to recommend to you for the purposes of this book. Remember, every bit of technical work you become embroiled in is a distraction from getting your show launched. I want you to launch your show, get the first ten episodes released, then put your fancy-pants on if you still feel as enthusiastic as you did at the start. All these finessed items can be introduced gradually, they don't all have to be ready from the get-go. I'd strongly recommend reading your intro and outro, making it part of your basic show format. No music, nothing fancy, just get on with it. The added advantage of this, as I found out myself, is that your show tends to evolve and find a level in those early days and what you pay somebody to record today probably won't still apply in ten episodes time.

Options 2 & 3 are technically simple, but they do have weekly time management and editing implications. If this is what you opt for, you're going to have to add these audio inserts at the beginning and end of each week's audio recording. That's a couple of extra steps and I automate this process using a service called Auphonic. Colin Gray also offers a service called Alitu which simplifies this process.

However, that's a podcasting ninja technique and not for this beginner's book. Unless you're happy and experienced with editing work and you can't get enough of the sight of sound waves on your desktop computer screen, let's opt for you reading your own intro and outro at the beginning and end of each episode. Script it too – no stumbles, ums and ahs in these important parts of the show. They're the first and last things people hear; make them strong, professional and confident.

Finding & interviewing guests

I spent most of my working days at the BBC – when I wasn't presenting shows – setting up and interviewing guests. I can't even begin to count how many people I've interviewed. Before I was a presenter, I was a radio reporter, and that involved me doing exactly the same thing, only I used to go out to interview the guests on location. I've recorded interviews hanging from a rope off the Humber Bridge, riding on a jet-ski, in a hot air balloon, on a light aircraft and with the fire brigade, in a burning room, experiencing a sofa fire simulation. I must have spoken to thousands of people on live radio, a mixture of 'regular' folk and 'famous' folk. I've had great guests, petrified guests, monosyllabic guests, self-promoting guests, offensive guests – every type of guest you can think of. On live radio you have to make it work; you can't just hold up your hands in the middle of an interview and say, 'Well this is rubbish' or 'We'll sort it out in the edit'. You have to work hard to squeeze out the juice.

I guess you can say I'm pretty experienced when it comes to finding and talking to guests. I'll share some practical interview techniques later in the book, but for now, let's talk about where the guests come from. How do you find interesting people to speak to for your podcast?

The first thing I'd say to you is that all guests are not equal. Some are used to speaking, happy to record with you and will fill your podcast episode with non-stop nuggets of information. With others it will be like mining for jewels in hostile terrain, pushing hard to prise every word out of their mouth. And some will um and ah so much, out of sympathy with the listener you'll be forced to edit more just to make it bearable on the ears. I'm telling you this for a good reason. Don't just book in *any* guest. Bad guests will make your life difficult and slow down your processing time. The guests I like best are those who turn up on time and allow me to record a one-take interview which I don't need to edit. As a former live radio presenter, I used to live in fear of the guest who would be so nervous they'd dry up mid-interview and need to be coaxed back into the world of the coherent.

I'd recommend that you prioritise guests who are 'on the circuit', people who are used to speaking and who won't be phased by the prospect. They don't have to have appeared on radio, TV or podcasts before – though that's nice. If they do talks in libraries or they're teachers or lecturers, these are all good signs. To be fair, most people who know about their topic will fall into these categories.

But what if you know somebody who'd be great in terms of their knowledge and expertise, but they've never done anything like a podcast before? In my self-publishing podcast, I've spoken to a fair few authors like that and they've been great, no problem at all. However, most of them have listened to my show beforehand, so felt that they 'knew' me already. We'd chatted online, I knew there was a resonance there. That helps a lot, it makes the process much less scary for them. The rest is about interview technique and how you come over as the show host. If you're terrified, disorganised and haven't got a grip, you'll convey that lack of confidence to your guest. They need to feel like they're in safe hands.

I once worked with a radio presenter who used to scare the life out of guests before she'd even spoken to them. She'd overwhelm them with so much detail about what was about to happen, it was a wonder they didn't run off and hide in a nearby cupboard.

I've got a BIG TIP that I honed after years and years of working in live radio, a tip so effective it's never broken out beyond radio's elite inner circle. I'm talking nonsense, of course, I wanted to make sure I have your attention. But my tip is to make your guest laugh. That's it. The sooner they laugh, the sooner they relax and start to relate to you as a human being rather than an interviewer. When I interviewed people face to face, I'd make them laugh, then hold their gaze – as you would in a normal conversation – distracting them from the fact that there was a microphone between us. But that's it; make 'em laugh. It relaxes people, you can see it in their faces.

If they're terrified by the prospect of you asking them questions, explain to them that it's a chat, not an inquisition, and that it should feel like you met in a bar or at a party and you're just having a relaxed chat about something they do for a living. It's no scarier than that.

Why did I tell you all that before I explained where to find the guests? Well, I want you to be picky about who you ask on your show. Bad guests are likely to make your listeners tune out and sometimes, no amount of editing can fix a terrible interview. Your aim as a podcast host is to select the right guest, not to book in anybody who says yes and has a pulse.

When I was at the BBC, we had a superb database of contacts and we could lay our hands on the records of the national radio stations too. We also had the clout (and the telephone numbers) to call places like the Houses of Parliament and book in politicians. When I was working at the BBC – and it wasn't all that long ago – we used a combination of the phone directory (remember that?) another paperback directory called the Hollis UK Press and Public Relations Annual (which doesn't appear to be a thing any more), and our contacts database. These days, life is sweet and it's a lot easier – we have social media.

How do you source and contact guests? Here's where I look:

- Listen to other people's podcasts and target guests you'd like to speak to.
- Connect with people in your industry on Twitter, LinkedIn & Facebook. Follow them for a while to get a good sense of whether they'd be a good fit as a guest.
- Who do you know already in your industry? Would they make a great guest?
- Seek out authors and bloggers in your niche.
- Read everything in your niche (see my earlier notes about Google Alerts and Feedly), and reach out to people who look like they have something interesting to say.

One of the things I learnt working with the BBC is that you should never think 'I'm too small, that person won't speak to me'. Podcasts give authors, experts and celebrities ongoing reach on the internet; once recorded an interview sits there forever, always ready to send a bit of web traffic their way. They love podcasters, so be aware of your value to them, it's not just a one-way street.

I contact virtually all of my podcast guests via social media. It's the podcaster's friend. Depending on your niche, Twitter, Facebook or LinkedIn might work best. I've used all three and they are incredibly effective. However, like all things, you've got to do it properly. So here are my practical tips:

- Always contact prospective guests by DM or direct message, never in a public post. Allow them to decline your invitation in private without feeling coerced into saying yes.
- Set up your social media profiles properly. If it looks like the dog chewed it, nobody is coming on your podcast.
- Get a proper, professional headshot on your social profiles. No sunglasses, swimming costumes, posing by sports cars, semi-clothed models of any gender or pictures of your cat, dog or hamster. I've seen all of these, except for the hamster. To coin a phrase – WTF? Just don't do it. Look professional and you'll be treated as a professional. Look like an amateur and they won't give you the time of day.
- Complete your profiles so that they introduce you as a podcast host and say a word or two about your expert experience. My author profile might say, *I am the author of 25 books, including 13 x thrillers, 10 x sci-fi and 3x non-fiction publications and host of the Self-Publishing Journeys podcast at PaulTeague.net/podcast* and a podcasting profile might read *I am a former BBC Radio presenter of 18*

*years' experience and host of the Self-Publishing
Journeys podcast at PaulTeague.net/podcast. A
veteran of more than 400 podcast episodes and
counting!*

- Get a professional banner for your social media
  outlets. Use free Canva.com to achieve this, it
  makes creating professional graphics a breeze.
- Set up a basic website if you can. We all check
  each other out online; if you haven't got a website
  you almost don't exist these days. Wix.com can
  be used for free and will give you a cool-looking,
  basic website in no time at all.

Finally, *what* you say when you reach out to guests is
really important. When potential guests reach out to me, I
won't even consider them if they haven't done their basic
homework. I expect them to have at least checked out my
show (they don't have to be able to list it as their Mastermind specialist subject), and have a good idea what type of
guest I'm looking for.

For instance, I present a show about self-publishing. If
you're a traditionally published author, you'd better have
come up with a good angle for me to justify including you in
my podcast. If I feel that you've sent me the same email as
500 other podcasts, you won't get a booking. In simple
terms, do the show host the courtesy of knowing a little bit
about them and building some resonance between the two
of you. Also, keep your email brief. I haven't got the time to
read War and Peace.

Here's an example of the sort of email I would send to a
potential guest who's never heard of me before:

Subject: Interview request for Self-Publishing Journeys podcast

Hi XYZ, I'm the host of the Self-Publishing Journeys podcast which features weekly interviews with writers who are making waves in the indie world.

I heard your interview with XYZ on the ABC podcast this week and was fascinated to hear how you managed to [insert impressive thing they did].

I would love to speak to you more about this as well as discussing your journey to becoming a bestselling author.

Would you be happy to appear as a guest on my podcast?
All interviews are pre-recorded, and I'll be happy to make the audio available for you to share on your blog.

If you're happy to do this, please book an interview slot via this scheduling link: [Scheduling link here]

Congratulations once again on [insert impressive thing they did] and I do hope we'll be able to talk for the podcast soon.

Best wishes, Paul Teague [insert link to your podcast]

That's it! Say who you are, why you want to speak to them, make a scheduling link available (more on this coming up) and sign off in a positive way. You don't need more than this. Make sure you include a link to your podcast so that they can check your credibility. That's it. It works, I've used that technique for years.

Always be friendly, brief, professional and to the point. Then wait for those bookings to roll in.

Pre-booking guests

I hate using the telephone. The only time I answer the phone – unless it's by appointment – is if it's my mum calling me. She has a hotline, nobody else does. My friends and family know to message me directly. Anybody else is probably wasting my time.

The reason I'm telling you this is to remind you that it's the 21st century. Tools exist to speed up our lives and I strongly recommend that you use them. The normal drill when you use the phone is that your call goes to voicemail or you disturb your prospect at a bad time and that makes it less likely that you'll get your interview. If they can be bothered, they call you back and get your voicemail. And so it goes on until you eventually manage to sort a date between you, or you just give up the will to live.

I use – and always have used – a scheduling tool, with inbuilt, automated reminders. That's why I've only ever had one no-show. And remember, he was a rare case of me accepting a pitch against my better judgement, so I probably should have known better anyway.

Scheduling tools link up with your online calendar and only make slots available to interviewees when you're free. You can never double-book. I use this system with consulting clients too, it works like a dream. When my prospective guest books in their slot, I get a notification. I confirm the slots and they get a templated confirmation note with a link to FAQs so that all their questions are answered (more on this ninja technique later). The software will then send reminders out at one day, three hours and one hour before our interview slot; and that's why I don't get no-shows. Except for that one bloke. Darn, that's annoying me now. He made me break my faultless run. He spoiled my brag. Curse him!

The tool I use is called OnceHub, but it does come with a small price tag. It's one of my favourite tools so I'll share it with you here. However, there are free scheduling services available, so I'd better give a couple a mention.

VCita is one I've played with on and off over many years, and it's a great place to start. VCita works with Wix and WordPress, my two preferred website creation services (though only look at WordPress if you have a budget or you like techie stuff). Calendly is the other free tool I have used and liked. To be honest with you, I can't even remember why I'm paying for a scheduling service now as vCita and Calendly are both very good. Another service that's on my radar is Acuity which gets good write-ups from several marketers that I follow. Any of these four options do the job and if you don't like them, do a Google search on *free online scheduling* and you'll find many alternatives.

Record an episode zero

Your episode zero is likely to be your most listened to episode over time. It's an important marker in your episode listings and enables any potential listener to get to grips with what you're about very quickly. It's basically the equivalent of your first day of induction in a new job, an audio approximation of showing you where the restrooms are, the kitchen and who parks where in the staff car park.

Here's what an episode zero should contain:

- A clear intro with show title and your name.
- A brief outline of who you are and your expertise/interest in the podcast theme.

- A brief overview of what the podcast will include.
- Ways to connect and get in touch – social media channels, website and email address.
- A teaser of what's coming up in your first episodes (make sure you can deliver these episodes before you promise them).
- A clear outro reiterating briefly what to look out for next and the timescale (i.e. look out for those first three episodes in your podcast feed from Monday 10th March).

Episode zero gets released as soon as your feeds are set up to Apple Podcasts, Google Podcasts etc. It can just sit there until you get launched, but this early release allows your feeds to propagate with that initial episode, giving you plenty of time to rectify any technical issues that may occur and to make your show discoverable ahead of its launch.

Once you have released your initial episodes, you can replace the original file in your episode zero and change everything except item six so that it remains timeless. The length of this episode should be very short – about five minutes.

Launch strategy

Ready to get this show on the road? You're going to need a launch strategy before you do that. You can't just release your first episode like it's a jelly flopping out of a mould. It needs some forethought to make the most of the resources that you have available. Now, if you're a massive celebrity already, none of this will matter. You can pretty well flop out anything like a wobbly jelly and it'll take off as your eager fans pounce to devour it. But for the rest of us, we're going to have to be a bit more creative. Here's my list of show launch considerations:

- What social media channels do you have at your disposal? LinkedIn, Twitter and Facebook are the best way to get the word out.
- Do you have an existing audience or a way to reach an audience? That might be a slot on somebody else's podcast, perhaps a weekly radio slot, newspaper column, a guest blog post, a newspaper interview with you or a group of trainees, colleagues or professionals who can help get the word out.
- Is what you're doing worthy of media coverage? Would the local paper/the Church magazine/the community newsletter/an industry publication be interested in mentioning your launch?
- Can you strategically target your first guests who have larger audiences than yours, so that they will share the episodes and get those initial downloads growing in number?

Think laterally about your initial launch and commandeer any resources that are available to you.

Stacking episodes pre-launch

The next thing I want you to consider is how many episodes you will release on launch day. We've already discussed episode zero and why it's important to have this episode in your rack. When I started Self-Publishing Journeys, I had ten interviews recorded and ready to release. I released episode zero ahead of the official launch day to make sure that the podcast feeds were set up correctly and the episodes were being picked up by Apple Podcasts, Stitcher and so on. Then I released three episodes at once, if memory serves me correctly, though it may have been five. How many you release is up to you but here's the concept: if I discover your new show, and I like it, I want to have more episodes available. When people discover your podcast, and enjoy it, they generally make their way through the back catalogue. Now, you don't have one of those yet, but it's wise to have a few episodes stacked up so that it looks like there's more of the good stuff still to come. Podcasters vary on how many shows you should make available on launch day, but I'd recommend three - five depending upon how organised you've managed to be in getting shows recorded upfront.

What if you're launching a news-based show? When we launched our crypto news podcast, we recorded several 'how-to' podcasts prior to launch. These outlined all the basics of cryptocurrencies and were the ideal content to have sitting there, as we gained audience; those introductory episodes were the ideal way to get started. So be creative, a series of onboarding episodes might be the best way to get around the issue if yours is a news-based show.

Every episode you release should be shared wherever you can find an audience. These days, social media is the best way to do this for most people who don't have a pre-existing platform. I'll discuss marketing and audience growth strategies in detail in a later chapter when I'll focus specifically on growing your podcast audience.

Time management & routine

I believe that your ability to manage your time will make or break your podcast. If you're a one-person whirlwind who leaves a trail of chaos wherever you go, good luck with that. Before long you'll be chasing your tail, behind with episodes and wondering if it's time to call it a day already. I'm not here to put you off – remember, I really want you to start and succeed with your podcast – but if you can't organise your way out of a paper bag, you're likely to struggle.

I run my show like a military operation. For a time, I was releasing three episodes each week: a self-publishing interview, a self-publishing diary and a cryptocurrency news show. I was also working three days per week and writing 10k words of a fiction book every seven days. To achieve all that, I work to a weekly planning schedule; I am meticulous in my planning. The simple truth is, if you can't manage to juggle several things at once – recording, editing and releasing this week's show while you're also booking guests for the month ahead – you're going to struggle. So, be realistic with yourself. If you are disorganised, that doesn't mean you have to throw the towel in. Maybe you can team up with somebody who has those skills. You might invest in a couple of hours of virtual assistant time each week. Get your kids to do it in exchange for a small bump in their pocket money. However, you do it, make sure you're set up to do this week in, week out.

I record my diaries at a set time each week, normally on a Friday afternoon, marking the end of my writing week. It's become embedded in my routine now; I feel strange if I'm not recording then. We recorded the cryptocurrency podcast on Thursday evenings, and I released the episodes on Saturday mornings, because I needed to give myself sufficient processing time. As I've already told you, interview episodes get a longer lead time because there's more that can go wrong with them.

Whatever you do, look at the pattern of your week and work out where you regularly have time available. If you have to give up some TV time, go for it. I carved out one hour each evening when I started working online, and that came from time I used to spend watching TV after work. What I have built up today started with one hour per day, while I was full-time working in a management role. That's how you can make these things happen. Plot spoiler! Sometimes effort is required.

Podcast episode release day

With all these matters attended to, you'll need to decide which day of the week to release your show. If your content is timeless, this won't matter very much. However, if your show is news-based, you may wish to release it into the world quickly, in case you're overtaken by events.

Here are my thoughts based upon personal experience:

- Monday has that 'start of the week' feel to it. I listened to Joanna Penn's podcast on my way to work every Monday morning for about three years; it became embedded in my routine. It always arrived on time and gave me a positive feel to the start of each week. I release interview episodes on Monday mornings.
- I have found from personal experience that Saturday release dates seem to be less competitive, meaning that my show turns up in the Apple charts more easily on that day. I

release my podcast diary on Saturdays and did the same with the cryptocurrency show for this very reason.

- Several shows that I listen to release new episodes on Wednesday and I'm always pleased about that because it gives me a choice of fresh content to listen to for the remainder of the week. I have released occasional self-publishing boot camps in the past and these were always scheduled for a Wednesday.

I'd recommend that you look at the competition as well when you're making this decision. Ultimately, it's all swings and roundabouts; the most important thing is that you pick a day – and time – and stick to it, releasing episodes on time, regular as clockwork.

Key points

- Think carefully about how you will deal with podcast interruptions like presenter illness, public holidays and day-to-day problems.
- Take time to work out the best way to intro and outro your show and consider where you will find guests if you opt for an interview format.
- Map out your launch strategy and consider recording an episode zero to get things underway.

7

RECORDING & EDITING YOUR PODCAST

Just as you can't make an omelette without breaking eggs, you can't make a podcast without using some software services. Although I've already told you about the best method, I know of to begin your new show for free, using Anchor, even that requires using an online service. And if you go for that option, it's likely that you'll need one of the tools that I outline below up your sleeve for a rainy day.

I use – or have used – all of these products and services. It's a big world out there in internet land, so you may read about alternatives elsewhere, but this is the list of favourites that I have gathered together in my time as a podcaster.

Skype

You've probably heard about this service already, but did you know it's an essential podcasting tool? Much as I hate to admit it, Skype is the most universally used and recognised tool for computer-to-computer communications, even though I'm convinced it was easier to use in the bad old days of dial-up internet – yes, I really have been using it that long. Skype is great for recording interviews and the audio quality is of a standard that we once had to use expensive ISDN lines to achieve when I was working in radio. You can also telephone via Skype, so it remains a 'belt and braces' tool which you can always wheel out in an emergency though you will have to use it with one of the software services that I outline below in order to record that audio.

I have used Skype for the majority of my interviews and, interestingly, the only two interviews I had technical issues with were one in Los Angeles which kept dropping out and one in my home county of Cumbria; I ended up finishing that interview on the telephone!

You won't need Skype if you're recording a solo show; Anchor will suffice for those purposes. However, it can be used for multiple presenter show formats and has the added advantage that you can use it with video too, so you can see your guest or co-hosts.

If ever I'm having problems with the connection, I usually turn off the webcam view and close a few tabs in my browser; it means that more of the resources on your desktop computer are available to take care of that Skype feed, and it can sometimes help if you are struggling with the audio quality of your call.

Depending on the audience for your podcast, and their level of technical ability, Skype is something that all but the very technical resistant know how to use. It's free too. Make Skype your friend. Download it to your desktop computer or laptop and it's ready to go if you ever need it.

MP3 Skype Recorder

This is the simplest, most reliable Skype recording tool that I have found, and it's saved my life with messed up podcast interview recordings on more than one occasion. It's a free software, and it downloads to your desktop computer or laptop.

MP3 Skype Recorder is free for personal, non-commercial use with a capped recording time of 30 hours per month. To be fair, the paid upgrade is so cheap, I'd recommend buying that, as I have done, just so that you can use the service without restriction and support the developers in keeping the service updated and available.

Once downloaded, MP3 Skype Recorder automatically records every Skype call. You don't have to remember to press 'record' or anything like that, from the moment your call connects, your voice and the voice – or voices – of your guests, are recorded in an audio file which is saved into a folder of your choosing. By the way, you can switch off auto-recording if you want to, but I leave it on; it means I never fail to capture an interview. I once had a critical error on my desktop computer and still managed to get my interview back from MP3 Skype Recorder. It really is the podcaster's friend.

Free vs. paid

Just a quick word about free versus paid-for services. Whenever you commit to a service, ask yourself how it gets funded and paid for. I hope you're making a long-term commitment to podcasting and that means you need to use services which are going to be around for a long time. Imagine how disruptive it would be if the service which hosts your podcast were to go out of business? For that reason, I recommend that you opt for software and services which have a funding model, whether it be via subscription or advertising. Services have to be paid for somehow – few people can afford to work for free – so it's perfectly reasonable that charges should be made. In this age of free, it's not always the cleverest option when setting up a podcast. So do take a little time to check that whatever you're using has some way of paying the bills. It's not a guarantee that the business will survive, but nobody can survive on fresh air alone.

Zencastr

Zencastr is the tool that I want to love and use but, at the time of writing, it's not quite there yet for my purposes. Consider it as an alternative option to Skype. I've tried it a couple of times, and I know other podcasters who use it for their shows, but the planets haven't yet aligned for me to make regular use of it.

Zencastr is a clever and inspired idea; it records each participant in an interview situation directly onto their own desktop computer (i.e. in perfect audio quality) then uploads those two audio files to its servers and 'stitches' them together so that they're synchronised. What you get is an interview that sounds like you're sitting in the same room.

Now, a technical point needs to be made here. If you have recording problems with Skype or Zencastr it's usually due to your broadband speed. However, that has caused some issues for me when testing Zencastr in the past. Also, if your podcast audience is not a technically sophisticated one, they may be more comfortable with Skype.

Zencastr is free for limited use and I urge you to take it out for a spin to see if it meets your requirements. The free option is particularly suitable if you have a regular co-presenter who is based in a different location. It's also good for single-guest interviews at the free level if your guests are generally happy to use unfamiliar web tools. Zencastr is extremely easy to use, but often with less technical podcast guests, Skype will be your safest option.

Mac options

I'm not a Mac user, but I'm aware that many of you reading this book will be. Although I can't personally vouch for these services, I can steer you in the right direction.

Squadcast allows you to record calls via your browser and, as such, that makes it device neutral. This comes at a cost I'm afraid, so will not be the best option for everybody.

Call Recorder by ecamm is a popular choice, it does have a small one-time cost and comes as a downloadable software for Macs.

Mac users can also record calls directly from Skype, so don't overlook the obvious in your hunt for a solution.

Audacity

I'm going to start by telling you that I don't like Audacity and I don't use it, but I feel duty-bound to tell you about it. There's absolutely nothing wrong with it, it's free, robust, it works perfectly well; it's just a hangover from my broadcasting days, I'm afraid.

Most people seem to think that broadcasters use super hi-tech editing software with every bell and whistle known to mankind. That certainly was not the case during my career, even though for more complex recording situations, clearly those advanced options were available. I spent my broadcasting career recording and editing interviews at a great rate of knots. There simply wasn't time to mess around and make mega-mixes. When I worked at BBC Radio

Humberside in the 1990s, I presented two live news shows, one running from 1-2 pm, the other from 5-7 pm. My shift started at 11 am, after the news team had held their meeting and confirmed the story prospects for the day. I had two hours to get briefed on what was coming up at one o'clock, record and edit any interviews that I had to do beforehand, fix up any guests that were needed and to liaise with reporters about their news stories. I had to write my own headlines, pull together my scripts and make sure I sounded calm, controlled and collected by the time I was live on air.

I have been recording interviews and editing them five minutes before a show went live. I have even recorded interviews during the news bulletin, listening to the newsreader on one side of my headphones to make sure I was back on time. How much time do you think we had for editing in that scenario?

I would present that live show until 2 pm, take a late lunch break, then we did it all over again, this time pulling together a two-hour live news show. I had a great team around me, I didn't do it all myself, but it was high pressure and we had no time to mess about with editing work that was too time-consuming.

That's a long way of telling you why I prefer simple editing software which allows me to make any edits that are required fast and easy, just like when I was banging out 15 hours of live radio, week in, week out. Audacity, for my tastes, is too fiddly. I used it in my early days of working online, but I never got on with it. So why am I taking up valuable words telling you about it? Well, it's fair to say that most podcast guides will recommend Audacity as the best, free software to use for audio editing. My dislike of it is very much due to my personal taste and preferences, so I don't want to deprive you of taking it out for a spin yourself; you might love it, after all.

Camtasia

I'm going to stick my neck out once again and say loud and proud that Camtasia is – and always has been – my preferred tool for recording and editing my podcast episodes. With the exception of a handful of shows which were recorded and edited whilst on holiday and away from the loving embrace of my regular desktop computer, I edit everything on Camtasia. However, it comes with a hefty price tag, which is why I'm offering you several alternatives in this chapter. It also offers PC and Mac options.

Camtasia is primarily a screen recording software which allows you to capture slide presentations and practical demonstrations on your desktop computer, then edit that recording and send it to YouTube, or various other publishing options. Initially, I bought it so that I could create internet marketing training products. I launched several of those products in my early years of self-employment and hammered my installation of Camtasia. But what I quickly realised is that it can be used to edit and record audio too – and the audio editing tool works exactly like the system I was using at the BBC at the time I left the corporation. It was simple, not overcomplicated with options that nobody ever uses, very easy to zoom in closely and make a fine edit, and reliable. I have been using and upgrading that software for over a decade now; it's exceptional for me to stick with a particular desktop computer tool for that length of time.

By the way, Camtasia has a useful setting which allows you to record system audio. That means you can record guest audio from a Skype call, as well as your own voice and because Camtasia records them as two separate tracks, where you have bad quality on your guest's Skype connection, you're able to tidy that up as part of the editing process.

You can download a free, one month trial of Camtasia and I recommend that you take Techsmith up on their kind offer. I must stress that you do not need to invest in a software at this price level to be successful in podcasting. I take the financial hit because it's what suits me best personally and because I also make heavy use of the screen-recording option. Don't even consider it as an option if you're starting on a restricted budget. Remember at all times, the success or failure of your podcast will not be determined by how much money you spend on setting it up, but the quality of content, and the passion and knowledge that you bring to the topic.

NCH Wavepad

NCH Wavepad is the closest, cheapest software I've found that is similar to Camtasia, but which can be purchased for a fraction of the cost. It's been around for years; it is robust and reliable and does a good job without overcomplicating matters.

The other reason I like this software is because it comes with an app version for your phone and this is what I used to edit a one-off episode from the beach at Benidorm while I was staying there one year. The app works well, so if you'll need to use your phone to record and edit away from home on a regular basis, it's worth considering the app and software combo, so that you can learn one editing system and get used to it.

Twisted Wave

On a couple of occasions, I've been abroad, listened to a pre-scheduled podcast on my phone, heard an error and then been left wondering how I'm going to make an edit when I'm hundreds of miles away from my trusty desktop computer. When I travel, I take a lightweight Chromebook, so whatever solution I use has to be browser-based, rather than a downloadable software.

Enter Twisted Wave, a rather fabulous browser-based tool which works superbly. Not only does it provide a simple, easy-to-use editing interface, it allows you to save your audio securely to your Google Drive account.

You can use it for free, but only for very short audio clips. I have tended to pay a couple of dollars each time I need to use it, then cancelled my subscription until I need it next. It's very cheap to use and is another of those services which is worth having tucked up your sleeve for emergencies.

By the way, Twisted Wave also makes a version for Macs. If you're a fan of Apple products, you may wish to check that out too.

Zoom

I discovered Zoom quite late in my podcasting career and it's what I used for my year-long cryptocurrency podcast. That show featured two presenters, both of us in different locations. I also wanted to try a video format and Zoom is particularly suitable for this. It is a combination of a Skype alternative – in that it records an audio file – and a Hangouts and Facebook Live alternative, in that it will record your webcam feeds too.

We used Zoom to record that show for the year of its existence and it never let us down. I set up a repeating event – we recorded at the same time every week – and we would join the 'meeting room' via the designated weblink. We used our webcams and microphones and Zoom recorded a video file and an audio file for us. Zoom arranges the presenters side by side on the video screen and it looks very neat when you see the final result. You can also use Zoom for multiple presenters, and it still lines the webcams up beautifully to create a single video output.

If you're using Zoom, unless you never have to make an edit, it's likely that you'll need to use a tool such as Camtasia which, of course, allows you to easily edit audio and video. When I processed the crypto podcast, I would sort out the video first and create the mp4 file to add to YouTube as a scheduled post. I would then output exactly the same file as audio only. It all worked like a dream with Zoom.

At the time of writing you can use Zoom for free as a basic user, but you are limited on recording time.

One final tip if you use this service; it's worth paying a little bit of money so that you don't have to worry about recording time limitations. Using it week in, week out, I found this to be the most robust way of setting things up.

Hangouts and Facebook Live

Some podcasters choose to use Google live streaming products or Facebook Live. I have experimented with both formats over the years, but I'm not a fan of either unless you have a ready-made audience who can join you there. I find the joining process less than satisfactory and you have to download the video file at the end of the live session and then process for the podcast channels.

Facebook Live is an excellent tool if you already have a decent fan base on that platform. Google Hangout style options never really worked for me, for personal or broadcasting use, so I'd generally advise giving them a wide berth. In my opinion and experience, Zoom is a much more manageable tool, even if it does come with a small expense.

Hindenburg

Hindenburg Journalist is another audio editing option which is popular, and it comes with a mid-range price tag. It offers a 30-day trial, and I did take it out for a spin once, but I still prefer my trusty Camtasia.

You're paying a lot of money to access the super-cool features and my advice would be to give this a wide berth until you've gained more experience and perhaps, you're beginning to ramp things up a bit. Definitely not for novices.

Other podcast software

I have offered options for every budget in this section, yet there's a whole world of different software and tools out there, many of which I have never heard of. I don't for one minute claim to know every bit of kit that's available, but I have gathered quite a collection of tools that I've used over the years.

It's worth a mention for Mac users that you have access to Garage Band as a built-in audio editing tool, but it's really designed for recording music, and can be a bit complicated for podcast purposes. However, it is an option to do your editing in iMovie and then just export the audio for the podcast. If you're tight on budget, but you use a Mac, this might be a decent working solution for you.

I'm sure you'll be aware of editing software like Adobe Audition too, a higher-end audio editing option. Well, good luck if you try to use it; to master a software with as many bells and whistles as that will distract you from what should be your core aim – to launch your podcast as soon as possible, without great expense or delay. You simply don't need something as complicated as this. There's nothing wrong with the software, a basic podcast just doesn't require this level of technical intervention. Remember, if your podcast is rubbish, it won't matter how much super-duper, mega audio processing you've done to it to get it out there; nobody will be listening anyway. There's all the time in the world to improve your skills and develop and enhance your podcasting process. But first, let's get the initial batch of episodes live so that the world can start to consume your amazing content. It all starts with that; not how expensive your software is. That goes for Adobe Audition and anything else you may discover out there on the internet.

Key points

- Skype and MP3 recorder make a great combo for recording remote guests, with Audacity as a free and popular editing tool.
- Camtasia is my personal favourite editing software, but it comes with a hefty price tag.
- Zoom is my preferred choice for recording multiple guests and presenters in different locations with the added advantage that you can also record in video format at the same time.

8

PODCAST PRESENTATION TIPS

This is where I get to roll out some of my best radio tips. Now, this is very much a case of *do as I say and not as I do*. Any kind of audio or video work that isn't highly produced is always going to be a case of doing your best in the moment. Don't beat yourself up too much about presentation. If you listen back to a show, and hear yourself doing something embarrassing, clock what it is and try not to do it again. You're already miles ahead of people who never even released their first episode, so focus on the important stuff before giving yourself a hard time.

I've been doing this for years; I still make the same mistakes – even though I should know better – and there's never a podcast that goes out where I don't think there's considerable room for improvement. These tips are offered in the spirit of encouraging best practice. No one show is likely to be perfect, but that doesn't mean we can't try for it. If you've never done this before, your early attempts may feel clunky, a bit wooden and perhaps even faltering. Keep going, push on and before you know it, you'll be able to hear how much you've improved. The same goes for presentation as it does for technical equipment; within reason, so long as you can present to a reasonable level, people care more about *what* you say than *how* you say it. If they like your show, they'll forgive you many things. So, sit back, switch on your microphone, relax and let's get presenting.

It's your voice, get over it!

If I had a dollar for every time an interview guest told me they hate the sound of their own voice, I'd be a billionaire by now, sipping cocktails on the beach in some exclusive resort. Everybody hates the sound of their voice. I hate the sound of my own voice. Everybody thinks they sound weird when they hear their voice back. It's part of the deal; get over it.

When you become a podcaster, you have to get used to your voice being the tool that you use. It's the only one you've got, unless you're some remarkable impressionist, so move on as fast as you can. Try to be objective about it, you're unlikely to ever like the way you sound.

When you go out into the world next, do a mental count up of how many people you speak to. Did any of them run away from you, claiming that your voice is so unusual they refuse to talk with you? Of course, they didn't. Everybody else accepts you the way you are, and they'll do just that on your podcast.

There are very few deal-breakers with this. Only a couple of weeks ago at the time of writing this very sentence I was discussing the setting up with a gentleman who had a physical disability. One of the results of this is that he had some difficulty with speech, and he was self-conscious about this. As we were chatting, I barely noticed, and it certainly didn't give me any problems understanding what he was saying.

I'm a big believer in the wonderful accessibility of the web; it's open to everybody and if you can make yourself understood in everyday life, I would encourage you to have a go, even if you feel self-conscious. Get your message out there. One of the things I said to this gentleman was, if he felt he needed to explain his minor speech impairment to listeners, to mention it once – perhaps in episode zero – then get on without further explanation. As far as I was concerned, the problem was in his own mind. His level of expertise in his chosen topic was excellent and it seemed a crying shame that he wouldn't share this in podcast form.

So please, take five minutes to tell yourself what a terrible voice you have then move on and never mention it again. Your voice is an essential tool; we all get the voice we're given. Treat it like any other piece of equipment; it's all that we've got to work with at this moment in time.

Presentation style

When you present your show, I want to implore you to be yourself. Don't try to sound like that imaginary hotshot radio presenter in your head, don't mimic somebody who you watch on the TV, just relax and be your natural self.

You have to show a bit of faith here. You have friends who like you, family who love you, acquaintances who are happy to pass the time of day with you. Relax, being yourself is enough, and just like your voice, it's all you've got.

If you try to pass yourself off as anybody else, it will come over as phony. Podcast listeners love the authenticity and closeness of the medium, make the most of it. You'll probably be surprised by how many people like you just the way you are.

Script or ad-lib?

I mentioned this earlier, but I want to reiterate it here; don't fully script your show. My worst nightmare as an interviewer on the radio was a nervous guest who scripted their answers beforehand. They sounded ridiculous. It probably seemed like a good idea at the time, but it always sounded abysmal on the radio. When a guest brought a script, I would ask rapid-fire questions so they couldn't follow it and force them to talk to me directly. That's all it is, after all, just a conversation between two people.

When you speak, it should sound natural, as if you're speaking to just me. It will sound anything but natural if you read out your words. So why do I advise scripting your intro and outro? Well, these are short and generally only basic info like the name of the show, your name, the episode number and the show title. This should be delivered in a natural, conversational way – not like you're delivering an academic speech to a room full of professors of science – and, when you get the hang of it, the transition between the scripted bit and the ad-libbed bit will become more seamless. It's important not to stumble or mess up that show intro and outro, that's why I recommend turning it into a brief script.

The best way to ad-lib is to write down bullet points of your conversation topics. Remember too that if you make too much of a mess of it, there's always the edit. You need to get used to talking and carrying on talking.

I was working with a client only last week who was getting excited about starting her own podcast but was expressing amazement at how I can open the microphone and speak for an hour without a script. This lady presents training days to rooms packed with attendees. I asked her if she started her training days from the beginning every time she stumbled over her words or forgot what she was about to say. Of course, she doesn't do that! She carries on, works her way around it and keeps on talking. That's what you do when you ad-lib.

If you struggle to do this it may be because you've chosen a topic that you don't know enough about. Have a think about that; you need to have a firm grasp of your topic to be able to talk about it without a script. If that's a struggle for you, just interview other people. That way, you ask the questions and they have to do most of the talking.

Ad-libbing around bullet points will always sound better. Add factual information and statistics to your notes too, you'll never remember that stuff. But all the linking bits in between, try to get used to busking those and remember that you can always edit it out later if it's too bad.

Microphone technique

Microphones can be tricky little devils. If you listened to what I told you earlier, you'll have a windshield and you'll have taken measures to place your microphone on a tripod or rubber mat so that it doesn't pick up all your hand movements.

Those are the basics; now you need to learn how to use the microphone correctly. I always wince when I see people who aren't used to using microphones placing their mouth directly in front of it, right up close. You wouldn't do that in somebody's ears so don't do it with a microphone. Think of a microphone like a pair of ears; too close and it's way too loud. Too far and we can't hear you. I position my own microphone about six inches or 15 centimetres away from my mouth. I naturally speak quite loudly and project strongly, so this is a comfortable distance for me. If you're very softly spoken, you may need to 'close-mic' it, so that the microphone is positioned just beyond your mouth. I used to do this when I'd been ill and my voice was hoarse, it meant I could hold out for the duration of a two-hour show.

If you laugh a lot, it's best to get used to moving back as you laugh, to give the microphone a fighting chance of being able to cope with the volume change. Always think of it like a pair of ears; did you just yell into my lughole? If you did, then back off.

When I worked in radio, we had to be hyper attentive to this and, to be fair, it's one of the most compelling reasons to use a mixing desk. On the radio, we used to do what's known as 'checking your levels'. We had two little meters, showing stereo output, each with a needle gauge showing a red and a green area. The needles would wag about as we spoke or played in interviews or music. Now, just think about it; if I blast the music on my radio show, and my voice is really quiet, you're going to constantly be turning the volume up and down. That's really annoying for the listener. Have you ever noticed how you have to turn down the TV when the adverts are on? It's because the levels are all over the place.

On the radio, we would do something called 'pre-fading'. You would check the highest audio level of a piece of music or audio, adjust the mixing channel accordingly, so that it fell within the safe green area on the dial and didn't force its way into the red. If it was in the red area, it was over-modulating; that's distortion to you and me.

You can't generally do this as a podcaster – not without a

mixing unit which gives you access to level meters – but as a single microphone show, or one that allows Zoom to manage the voice levels, that won't be a problem. If you have multiple voices, all in the same room, you're moving your show into the realms of a radio broadcast rig, and you'll need to take advanced advice on that. Podcast expert, Colin Gray is your man for that job, if you need him.

Camtasia has a simple level checker built into it and that's just one more reason why I use and love that particular software. In a simple way I can be certain that my audio isn't too loud and isn't too quiet. You're after an audio volume in the middle, basically, just as if you were speaking to somebody in the same room. It's the principle I want you to take away here – there is such a thing as too loud and too quiet, and you need to be mindful of both.

By the way, if you've ever been on the radio as a guest, this is why the reporter or presenter 'takes level' before you go live on air. In the old days they used to ask you what you'd had for breakfast that morning. They just wanted you to speak so they could adjust their levels. There's nothing worse than asking a guest the first question and you can't hear a word they say. If a presenter is doing their job properly, you should never have to adjust the volume on your radio as you listen; the sound should be even throughout the show.

Before you start recording episodes, if you've never done this before, I suggest that you practise recording and try different things. Before you speak, explain where the microphone was at the time. Your test audio might sound something like this:

Example 1: Very close to the microphone
Blah, blah, blah

Example 2: 15cm away from the microphone
Blah, blah, blah

Example 3: Sitting back in my chair whilst talking
Blah, blah, blah

Example 4: Laughing close to microphone
Ha, ha, ha!

Listen back and get a feel for how the sound changes as your position is altered. Get used to using the microphone before you record for real.

Another annoying habit for listeners is breathiness on the microphone. This usually means you're too close to it or, in the case of a headset, the mouthpiece is way too close. We don't need to hear every gargle of your throat, be mindful of this. Once again, running some tests will help to prevent these basic problems.

Finally, take note of your position relative to the microphone. Are you slouched or slumped down in your chair? Are you upright and able to move your hands as you speak? We want to hear your best self and your position whilst speaking will go some way to determining this. Some presenters stand up to give their show more energy; you might like to experiment with that. You need to sit in a way that makes you sound like you're not half asleep and one which will allow you to manage your breathing well.

As a general rule, sitting up straight in a comfortable chair will work well for most people. Please avoid slouching at all times when recording audio.

Things not to say

A lot of the points made in this section are my personal opinion, so take them with a pinch of salt if you disagree. They're not hard and fast rules, but I do urge you to give them some consideration.

This is a list of things not to say or do when you're presenting your show. I hear a lot of them on other podcasts and they annoy me. With that said, I have no doubt whatsoever that I will drive my podcast listeners spare with some of the things I say or repeat.

The simple strategy here is to listen back to your own episodes and do your best to pick up on your own annoying habits. I've done this for years, on radio and as a podcast host. I don't think for one minute that I always get it right but listening back to your work should help you target your worst habits, at least.

Here's the list of things to avoid, along with my thoughts for each point made.

How are you?

When you start an interview with a guest please don't start by saying 'How are you?'. It's pointless, we don't care, and it doesn't move things on. What happens is this:

How are you?
Fine, thanks. How are you?
Great thank you.

It's pointless and we don't need to hear it. Instead, get tucked into the meaty start. Begin with a question. These pleasantries need to stay in your pre-chat, we don't want to hear them in the edited version.

Without further ado

I also hear presenters using the phrase 'without further ado'. That's another phrase that drives me crazy. It suggests that what you've just been saying is trivial and a hold-up. I'm guessing it is neither of those, so why suggest that it is? And if it is trivial and pointless, maybe you shouldn't be including it in the first place. This is one of those annoying phrases that gets us nowhere, is overused and should be ditched without further ado.

No response

Many podcasts encourage questions or participation from listeners. If you haven't received any questions, don't tell us! I never want to hear you saying 'We haven't had any questions/entries/responses' because what's the implicit message of that? It suggests you have few or no listeners and very little audience interaction. This is like the magician giving away how a trick is done.

There were times on the radio when we'd get no – or few – callers for a phone-in show. You'd never have heard me saying 'We're getting no calls today' because that would have been advertising my failure. If you didn't get any responses, phrase it differently, so it doesn't sound like your show is on life support. Compare these two examples:

We haven't had any questions submitted this week, but if you do want to get involved, please email me at XYZ

I'd love to hear your thoughts on this subject, it's easy to take part in the show, just email me at XYZ

Example one sounds like Billy No-Mates, example two makes you sound like you have a hot and happening show.

The same goes for those podcasters who encourage support via Patreon, which I'll be telling you more about later in the book. I often hear presenters saying *We haven't got any new Patreon supporters this week*. That makes it sound like you just invited us to the world's lamest party. Big it up people, make it sound more exciting. As listeners we don't need to know that nobody supported your show this week. Instead, excite me about the prospect of supporting your show with something like this: *If you'd like to join our other Patreon supporters who are all receiving extra audio and bonus blog posts, head over to my Patreon page now and become a supporter of the show ...*

Always use active and positive language whenever your show is concerned.

Keep it simple

Keep your language simple and chatty. In my early days with the BBC, the older generation of listeners were convinced we used to sit there in dinner jackets announcing the news. These days, you'll hear regional accents, people with disabilities, and voices reflecting the wonderful diversity in our society. Well, hurrah to that, it's about time too. The days of posh blokes in dinner jackets are long gone. Speak how you speak naturally, don't feel like you need to put on your posh voice for your podcast. Use the language you use every day; your audience will thank you for it.

Many listeners are doing other things while they're

listening – you probably don't have 100% attention. Keep it simple and straightforward, they'll be able to follow you easier.

Jargon

Don't use jargon, abbreviations, in-jokes or acronyms. Always assume the show that you just recorded is the first that the listeners have heard; can they access everything easily or will they feel excluded? We had to take great care with this when interviewing guests on the radio. A guest might say something like *When soldiers go MIA ...* where MIA means missing in action. As a presenter I'd say *MIA which stands for missing in action* once, then I'd use MIA after that.

If I was interviewing you and you used an acronym I'd interrupt and ask you what MIA stands for. Just because you know, doesn't mean your guest does. You're the interviewer, you're in charge, if you think your listeners might not be clear, ask the guest to clarify.

I listen to a podcast which I enjoy greatly, but there are many in-jokes used. Each week they tell you to listen to the back episodes to have the in-jokes explained. Well, actually, I just want to know what the hell you're speaking about without having to go on a wild goose chase through the back catalogue.

If you have a lot of in-jokes, just create a simple written guide which acts as a glossary; it means I can access your show from the get-go and makes me feel like I'm on the inside. Incidentally, if your show thrives on in-jokes, you can turn this into a marketing tool by making your glossary available in exchange for an email address. More on this when we talk about marketing strategies.

Divisive topics

Steer away from divisive topics at all times. I strongly recommend you avoid the great dividers – sport, religion and politics. Now, if any of those three is your podcast topic, this rule does not apply. However, if you deal with some other topic on your show, just walk away from anything too controversial.

Mention football on a self-publishing podcast and I'd bet that more than half the audience will immediately enter a comatose state. They'd listen to a football podcast if they wanted to listen to football banter. It's best to stay on topic, I don't care what your political leanings are if I only listened because I wanted to find out how to groom my gerbil on your Caring For Gerbils podcast.

Rude guests

Don't let guests hijack your show. Allow guests to make a polite pitch, invite them to mention their new book, website or widget, but they are a guest on your show, and you need to ask them to refrain if they're over-plugging their product. This is sometimes best dealt with in your pre-chat with a guest. Explain to them that they'll be given an opportunity to plug their product at the beginning or end of the interview.

This is part of a reciprocal exchange; they want to use your audience for advertising, but they're your guest and they have no right to take over your show; that's just rude.

Advertising

I don't take advertising, but if I did, I'd want those adverts to be targeted and relevant. In my industry, Joanna Penn does this best. She only accepts advertisers who she has personal experience of and when she does the ad read, she relates the product to her own experience, which makes it all the more effective. Always keep related sales promos relevant and on-topic. Why would I want to hear about dog food on your gerbil show? Introduce me to the new mini hairdryer for rodents and I'm all ears.

Saying thank-you

Here's a final bugbear from my radio days – don't thank everyone because we don't care. I don't mean to be rude, but in the context of a radio show, it all got a bit wearing when presenters thanked the weather forecaster, the travel bulletin reader and the news anchor. And who even knows what the producer does? My rule of thumb is that we don't thank people who are just doing their job. In the context of a podcast, that means not thanking your co-presenter(s) for routine stuff. However, remember to always thank listeners for anything they do.

There's quite a list to chew on there, and I don't want you to get hung up on those items. When you're listening back to your shows, just ask yourself from time to time if something is annoying, superfluous, divisive or just plain irritating. We're always seeking more of the good stuff and much less of the bad stuff. You'll never get it perfect, just aim for as good as possible.

Repeating what we just heard in the jingle

If you decide to opt for the jingle route – with either a recorded voice introduction or a music and voice combination – please take care not to repeat what the jingles just told us. I hear this time and time again on podcasts – and yes, I do it myself too – but I really should know better.

Here's an example:

[Jingle] *Welcome to the ABC podcast - and here's your show host, XYZ ...]*

[Presenter] *Hi, I'm XYZ and welcome to the ABC podcast ...*

You just told us that!

Jingles serve a purpose in a show; they anchor it, they change the pace, they provide markers. Sometimes they give us information which you don't need to repeat. In radio, I used to have a variety of jingles at my fingertips, and we'd deploy these carefully to change the mood and pace. If I was moving from an emotional news item to a funny news story, I'd use a slow-to-fast music bridge. If I'd just been having a laugh about something and was about to switch to an important news story, I'd used a fast-to-slow music bridge to change the mood quickly.

Jingles serve a purpose; you don't just stick them in there for the sake of it. If the jingle just told us something, there's no need to say it again. You might only have said it once, but the listener – and remember, this is all about the listener – has heard it twice.

Recording environment

Always be aware of your recording environment and get used to closing your eyes and scanning your area with your ears. We need to think like a microphone. If you're recording at home, avoid anything that's making a noise. Persistent hums and taps are the worst offenders. Never ever, ever record with music in the background. Not only does it give you copyright issues, it's also impossible to edit against speech. You make the music error once. In the early days of my radio career, I recorded a live band playing, thinking I'd created a wonderful sound vista for the programme.

'Did you check to see if they were Musicians' Union?' the producer asked, like he'd seen it all before. Of course, I didn't check. And, surprise, surprise – I couldn't use the music. Because I'd recorded the interviews with the music in the background it was game over.

You're most likely to get caught out with this if you record a guest in a different location. Always insist music is turned off, even if you're in a hotel or restaurant. They'll do it, don't worry. I've asked for this many times in my life, both at the BBC and as a podcaster.

If you're recording in a workplace, at a conference or other noisy venue, try to find a place as far away as you can from the worst noise. 'Close-mic' the recording apparatus so it's a little closer to the main source of the sound i.e. your voice and your interviewee's voice. Ask yourself at all times: *What is the dominant sound here that the listener will pick up on*? If the answer to your question is not the interviewer's and guest's voices, reset the location so that it is.

Making apologies

Avoid repeating apologies, they just draw further attention to something we probably weren't even aware of anyway. If you need to apologise for something, say it once and move on.

Earlier in the book, I mentioned the gentleman who felt he had a speech impediment, one which I was barely even aware of. I told him that I didn't think he even needed to mention it, but if he did, say it once and move on.

Dogs and noisy families are a regular source of apologies. Most dogs I can't even hear on the audio, especially when they're just coming or going or having a shake, so I'd caution against describing their every move. If you need to tell us the dogs are in the room, say it once, then move on. We'll just assume any noises from that point onward are a dog, unless there's a goat you neglected to mention. Now, if the dog is barking constantly, that becomes a recording environment issue, as outlined in the previous section. This is an audio deal-breaker. Do whatever you have to do to sort out the barking – feed/walk/comfort/groom/sing to/stroke the dog and return to the podcast once the issue is resolved. It's the same with kids and families. If they're making a bit of a noise in the room next door, mention it once and move on. We know what kids sound like when they're playing. If they break down the door and start recreating a wild west shoot-out in your work room, we're back in the realms of recording environment; you know what to do about that by now.

If you've got a sore throat, if you're having to use a dodgy microphone because the usual microphone is broken, if you've had to record on the old Windows XP laptop because your regular desktop computer exploded, ask yourself the following: will listeners even notice? If the answer is yes, apologise once and get on with the show. If the answer is no, get on with the show. Whenever you can, just get on with the show.

I'll let you into a secret. My study is a box room at the end of the house. Just outside the door is the utility room in which is located a washing machine and dishwasher. I often record with the dishwasher on, but the door closed. Plot spoiler: you can't even hear it. If you can hear it, nobody ever mentioned it. I even record sometimes when the washing machine is on. But when it goes into its spin cycle, we're back to recording environment issues and I pause my recording until it's quietened down or mention it once and move on. Apply the dishwasher-washing machine model to your podcast and you can't go wrong.

Teasers and trailing ahead

Think of your podcast like a story; it should have a strong beginning, middle and end. I like teasers at the beginning of a show because they can often make a listener hang on until the end to hear what you were talking about. We're in show business here, we need to plan and behave like we know what we're doing.

Pace your content, remind listeners what's still to come, entice them, compel them to stay listening. Here are some examples:

'Don't forget, I'll be revealing my income figures for this month before the end of the show ...'

'We've still got that mega tip to come, when I'll let you know how you can make the same pizza that the Queen eats at Buckingham Palace for the price of a coffee at your local store ...'

'After a word from our sponsor, I'll announce the winner of this week's prize ...'

A great story keeps the reader engaged, actively listening and almost compelled to stay tuned in. Does your show plan look like a series of points to be trotted out in a particular order or have you applied the showbiz rules, to order and present it in a way that encourages better engagement from your listeners?

Idents and branding

This sounds like it's very corporate, but it's not really. Listeners need to know what your show is called so that they can review it and find it online. You have to achieve a balance between annoying regular listeners and concealing this information from new listeners. Radio presenters *ident* (radio shorthand for 'identify') all the time because you might not know which station you're tuned into, but podcast listening is more intentional; your listener generally downloaded your show and knows what they're listening to.

I'd recommend slipping it in in more subtle ways, without making a big deal of it. However, for basic branding purposes, please don't leave me wondering what I'm listening to. A strong intro with your name + show title, a subtle reminder or two during the show, and an outro which includes your branding is quite enough. Here's now I might manage that within a one-hour podcast:

- *Intro/jingle: Welcome to the XYZ podcast, the show which puts the GO! into goats. Here's your show host, goat racing expert and trainer, Billy Gruff ...*

- *At 20 mins: Let's move on and take a look at this week's XYZ podcast mailbag ...*
- *At 40 minutes: My guest now on the XYZ podcast is goat vet, Ivor Bleat ...*
- *Outro/jingle: Thanks for listening to the XYZ podcast – we'll have more goat goings-on for you next week. Until then, happy bleating!*

Okay, so that's a little tongue-in-cheek, but you get the point. Ident and brand your show, work it into the fabric of what you're doing so that it doesn't become too annoying.

In summary, you're unlikely to ever listen back to one of your shows and think that you were pitch perfect. The truth is, I've been doing this for years, and I still make basic rookie errors. My advice when it comes to presentation is as follows:

- Don't beat yourself up about it, just do it as well as you can.
- There's always a next time.
- There's always the edit.
- It gets easier the more you do it.
- Strive for constant improvement.
- Listen back to yourself, be objectively critical, but also don't be harsh with yourself.

Key points

- One of the biggest hurdles you'll face as a podcast host is getting used to the sound of your own voice. Regard it as an essential working tool, nobody else will be bothered about it.

- Take some time to experiment with and master microphone technique.
- Learn about the pitfalls of being a presenter and resolve to review your podcast performance so that you're always striving to improve.

9

REFINING THE PODCAST PROCESS

You've probably figured out by now that I'm a firm believer in systems and processes. There's no way I could produce the amount of output that I do – in terms of podcast episodes and books – if I wasn't super-organised. I have a highly-refined and fully-automated podcasting process which makes my life as easy as it can possibly be. Everything is templated, systematised and replicable in order to spare me the torture of having to repeat the same processes every week. Other than getting somebody else to do all the work, this is the most finessed way that I have found to run and produce podcasts, and I'm happy to share it with you here. I haven't seen most of these tips in any other podcasting book before. You're welcome!

Automated guest booking

I've touched on this already, but if you're using a guest format, you must introduce automated guest booking to speed up your process. In case you missed it, use OnceHub, vCita, Calendly, Acuity or search Google for something that you like better.

Make sure your online calendar is up to date and if you're batch-recording guests, leave a half-hour buffer between interviews to keep you fresh/go to the loo/allow for over-runs/grab a bite to eat or a drink.

Use the built-in reminders to prompt the guest at regular intervals – I go for three days/one day/one hour or one day/one hour/ten minutes. Include a link to your guest FAQ too. More on which in the next section.

Automated booking is a thing of great beauty and a massive time-saver.

Guest FAQ pages

This tip will spare you so much to-ing and fro-ing with guests. It's a simple web page which is titled *Podcast Interview Guidance*. On this page, I introduce myself and answer all possible questions about the podcasting process. Having interviewed a fair few guests now, the concerns and queries are usually easy to anticipate:

- What questions will you ask me?
- What equipment will I need?
- Is it live? Can you edit it?
- When will my interview go live?
- What should I expect on the day? How will this work?

I have shared the full text of my guidance page below, so that you can adapt for your own purposes. By the way, the headset I recommend has an affiliate link on it which means I make a small amount of income every time a guest buys a headset through my link, at no additional cost to them. It's a headset I use myself, so I'm happy to recommend it. I'll say more about affiliate links later in the book, but always be on the lookout for monetisation opportunities which will help to pay for any costs incurred in setting up your show.

I include the weblink to this FAQ page in every one of my automated reminders about our scheduled interview.

Interview guidance page (example text)

Thank you very much for agreeing to record an interview for Self-Publishing Journeys, I really appreciate it!

I thought it would be useful to jot down the answers to some basic questions, to help set the scene for our Skype chat.

What I need from you

Important! Please would you let me know your Skype name and send it to me by email to [EMAIL ADDRESS].

My Skype username is [INSERT SKYPE HERE] – please feel free to send a contact request.

What's the deal with this podcast?

Self-Publishing Journeys launched on Monday 4th April 2016.

The joy about this type of interview is that it's evergreen, the value holds over time and when people discover and like a new podcast, they tend to listen to all of the back episodes.

Podcasts are a great thing to get involved in … and you can use the interview audio on your own website too.

What topics will you cover?

It will focus, in the first instance, on authors (and those who support them) who are in the early stages of their careers.

Most of the interviews will be with self-published authors, but it's important to be aware of all the options, so I do go off-piste occasionally.

In general, I want to hear from the next/upcoming generation of authors.

If you're an established author, I will dig deep into your personal journey and how you overcame the inevitable hurdles.

Interviewees must have published at least one book and have made some sales; it doesn't matter how many.

They need to be able to talk through their processes, problems, solutions, concerns and successes as a writer.

I'll also be including support experts in my guest list, so that new authors can learn about things like book cover creation, proof-reading, copy editing, author platform building, PR strategies and so on.

Research

I've checked you out already online – or we've already met – as I wouldn't have invited you to be a guest otherwise i.e. I'm already familiar with the basics of your publishing experience.

I prefer not to know too much before we chat, it keeps the flow more natural.

I won't have read your books (probably) but this is not a book review podcast, I want to know about how you write, why you write what you do and how you produce and sell your books.

However, if I need a little more info about you, I'll email you directly.

Similarly, if there's something that I need to know, or mention, please tell me in our interview pre-chat when we first connect via Skype.

How will my interview go live?

I record several weeks ahead of the release date.

Most times, I'll give you a date at the end of our Skype interview.

I'll send you a link to the page and a screenshot to allow you to suggest any changes before it gets published.

How will you access your own interview?

I'll be publishing the interviews on this website using a special audio player, which allows you to generate the HTML code to easily embed the interview into your own blog.

If you want to download the mp3 file, you'll be able to do that via the player console.

Download links are located at: [INSERT WEB LINK]

Accessing your file is simple; as soon as your podcast episode goes live, you'll be able to get your hands on it.

I'm not used to doing this! What sort of questions should I expect?

Interviews will be about 50 minutes in duration and will be conducted via Skype, audio only.

The format will be very informal and chatty, please don't get anxious if you've not done this before.

You should definitely not read from a script; it will sound terrible.

Just relax, follow my lead and treat it like we're chatting on the phone.

However, if you need to make a few notes as reminders – web addresses, book titles and so on – that's fine; I have a memory like a sieve and will be doing the same.

Here are some examples of the type of question that will be asked:

– What is your background?
– What made you start writing?
– Why self-publishing?

– What were the hardest self-publishing tasks that you had to master?

– What tools do you use to produce your books?

– Any learning points to pass on to newbie self-publishers?

– How do you market your books?

– What do you wish you knew more about to make self-publishing easier?

I never stick to the questions, so please don't ask me for a list of what I intend to ask beforehand.

I'll be treating it like a regular conversation and the best conversations flow naturally.

Do I need to worry about any technical matters?

It will help if you have an external microphone, rather than one that is built-in, to ensure that the recording quality is good enough.

If you don't have an external microphone, please let me know beforehand, it's not always a deal-breaker.

I will dial into Skype at the appointed time and I will take care of the technical matters.

All you have to do is to relax and chat.

Use headphones please, or it will generate a terrible sound quality.

Want to be a 'Pro' podcast guest?

If you'd like to be a guest on other podcasts, as well as mine, here's a tip!

Always have a decent microphone and always use headphones.

You owe it to yourself (and the podcast host) to make sure that the audio quality is as good as possible.

Here is my recommendation for the cheapest, most basic level of microphone & headphone combo if it's time to invest in a bit of decent equipment.

There's much better available, of course, but this will make sure that you're sounding good when the interview is recorded.

[INSERT AFFILIATE LINK FOR Logitech H390 USB Headset]

What else do I need to know?

We'll have a brief pre-chat before I start to record the interview, just to make sure the sound is fine, and you have time to tell me about anything that you want to mention.

I'll tell you when I'm going to start recording, so you'll know when what you say is 'on the record'.

I'll lead the way with the questions, I won't ask you anything that you can't answer, all you have to do is to treat it like a regular conversation.

At the end of the interview, I'll thank you for being a guest, then ask you where we can check you out online.

This is a good time to mention your blog/website, Facebook business page and/or Twitter account.

Don't list more than three outlets, people will lose the plot.

Important: Rights Issues

The rights to the interview are mine, though as the interview guest you may also use the audio as you please so long as I get a credit and reciprocal web link.

I will also credit and link to you in any of my uses of the interview.

I may transcribe interviews for future use, if so, you may have a copy, at no charge.

Important: Editorial Control

Final editorial control and decision-making are mine as the publisher of this content.

That won't cause you any problems at all and I'm always happy to edit out bits if necessary, at your request.

However, the final judgement resides with me.

I also reserve the right not to run an interview – because it will require too much editing, because the audio quality was too bad, because there are too many legal issues, because you turned it into a pitch-fest or because I don't think it's right for my podcast brand.

It's very unlikely that will ever happen, but it's worth me flagging up from the get-go.

My aim at all times is to make you sound great and to provide a useful interview for our listeners.

The legal obligations are mine too, so I will remove anything which may cause problems in that area.

It's worth me mentioning my Disclosure & Endorsement Policy too: [INSERT WEB LINK HERE]

That page outlines my approach to 'plugging' or promoting services or products, though you may mention your own books and products in passing of course.

What next?

Once we're finished, I'll check that the interview is fine then we're done.

I'll follow up by email to confirm your interview release date.

Post-interview info

Once you've finished recording your interview, you'll conclude by telling your guest when their interview will go live and how to find and share it. Now this is definitely something you must do, as it will help you to strategically grow your audience.

Rather than write the same email to every guest, I use a feature in GMail called Canned Responses. If you're not using GMail yet, it's time to make the switch. It's the marketer's friend for all sorts of reasons I'm not going to expand upon here, but for the purposes of this book, Canned Responses are your friend.

In simple terms, they allow you to create, save and reuse a templated email without having to cut and paste it or format it every time. You can save as many Canned Responses as you need and they're very handy whenever you find yourself having to write pretty well the same email more than three times in a row. With over 140 guests and counting, this technique has now saved me a lot of time.

Your post-interview email should meet the following requirements:

- Thank the guest.
- Confirm when their interview goes live.
- Send them a link to their show notes page – I always ask them to check it too, in case I got anything wrong.
- Encourage them to share the episode.
- Thank them again.

Interview follow-up email (example text)

Hi NAME

Thank you very much for recording an interview with me for Self-Publishing Journeys, I really appreciate it.

As promised, here are the details of your broadcast date and promotional page link.

Please note that the page link below will not be published until 05:00 on your go-live date.

Your 'go-live' day is: Monday DATE

Your page link to share will be: [WEB LINK]

I have attached a screenshot (below) of what your page will look like.

Please let me know if a) you'd like anything to be changed on the page b) it's okay to use the photograph that I have used for copyright purposes.

When the audio goes live, you will be able to access the files via this link: [INSERT WEB LINK HERE]

You can download the audio file there, get the code to embed the interview on your website or easily share the recording on social media.

Thank you once again for taking part in the podcast, I really appreciate your contribution.

Best wishes,

Paul Teague

Google Drive/Website show templates

I create all my show notes in Google Drive, which is free. I have a show template – which I already showed you in a previous chapter – and I mass produce that template in

Google Drive by using the 'make a copy' function. Not only does this save me lots of time, it also means all scripts are available and saved in the cloud, so I can search for info that I need and may have forgotten, however old that show script is.

I tend to create the show script formats in batches of 20 or so, that keeps me going for quite some time. All I have to do is add in the dates and I'm good for the next four - five months.

I do the same for my show notes. Now, this only really applies if you're using WordPress for your website – or something very similar to it – but I keep a templated show notes page in draft form in my WordPress website. I use a free WordPress plugin which allows me to clone pages and posts – just do a search for the word *clone* in the plugins area – and I clone 10-20 new show notes pages at once, inserting the date and any bespoke information for that episode. My show notes format matches my web page format, so I can often cut and paste the information over from one to the other.

In all situations, I am trying to avoid duplicating work, and I refine this process whenever I can.

Web page show notes (example text)

Welcome to Paul's Podcast Diary for DAY + DATE + YEAR. Coming up this week:

1)
2)
3)

This diary charts my self-publishing journey - the ups, the downs, the successes and the failures.

Everything goes into this diary, week-by-week, but you'll also find it a source of great tips, resources, tools, podcast recommendations and so on.

If you're new to the podcast and want to easily access the back catalogue of podcast diaries, in chronological order, please check out this page.

If I ever miss something out, or you'd like more information, just drop me an email at ME@MYEMAILADDRESS

[LIBSYN AUDIO EMBED CODE GOES HERE]

This Week's Talking Points

1)
2)
3)

This Week's Mentions

1)
2)
3)

You can access every episode of Paul's Podcast Diary, in chronological order, here. [WEB LINK TO PREVIOUS DIARY EPISODES]

Canva templates

If you haven't discovered Canva yet, I'm about to change your life. Never again will you have to use complicated image editing software. Canva is free – with a paid option available should you want it – and it will allow you to do the following:

- Create all your podcast show and web graphics without any fuss or technical stuff.
- Create correctly sized promo images for Twitter, Facebook, Instagram and any other popular social channels.
- Give you access to licensed photos, templates and graphics.
- Allow you to create correctly sized YouTube thumbnail graphics.
- Allow you to batch produce graphics by deploying the duplicate feature.

Canva is the podcaster's friend, you will be able to batch produce weeks' worth of show graphics. I have used the free option for several years now, it's a tool that I use almost every day.

Outsourcing

If you're going to get more done in less time as a podcast host, I highly recommend that you become acquainted with outsourcing. This is where you pay somebody else to manage the tasks that you have to do. You can use it on a job-by-job basis, or you can employ a full or part-time virtual assistant who works alongside you in the business, albeit usually somewhere else in the world.

I outsource work frequently and I've outsourced some unusual things in the past:

- My podcast graphic design was outsourced.
- The cover for this book was outsourced.
- I once outsourced translation of a book advert from English to Chinese.
- My podcast jingle voice-overs were outsourced.
- I once created an entire software using the services of an excellent outsourced coder who I never met in person.
- I hired a salesman to make direct calls on my behalf.

You should use outsourcers to do the following tasks:

- Jobs you can't do yourself.
- Job you don't want to do.
- Routine, time-consuming tasks which are not a good use of your time.

The best book that you can buy on this topic is *Virtual Freedom* by Chris Ducker. It will give you chapter and verse on how to outsource like a pro. To get you underway quickly, here are websites that every outsourcer needs to know about:

Service: Fiverr

Weblink: fiverr.com

My notes: I use this all the time for 'micro' jobs which are sweet, short and simple. Prices start at $5 and treat it like eBay; look for well-used services which have lots of positive reviews. If you're getting graphics work done, always confirm with the vendor that you have copyright clearance to use the image. If in doubt, you buy the image and send it over to the contractor.

Service: People Per Hour

Weblink: peopleperhour.com

My notes: This is a good site to use for more substantial jobs, I have used it successfully on many occasions. I once paid a contractor to show me how to set up and operate Google retargeting, recording the session as a tutorial. This was money well spent, I have used this new skill many times since.

Service: Upwork

Weblink: upwork.com

My notes: This is the site where I found the excellent coder who built my software service. What a great discovery he was. I paid thousands of dollars of invoices through this site and found it excellent for sourcing great talent and managing the financial elements of more demanding projects.

Key points

- Apply time management techniques such as automated guest booking, page templating and creating FAQ pages.
- Try outsourcing if there are certain tasks that you'd rather not do or if you don't have the skills you need in some areas.
- Try to deploy systems in your podcast preparation, this will increase the chances of your show's survival.

10

PODCAST INTERVIEW ESSENTIALS

Having conducted what must be well over a thousand interviews in my broadcasting career – and possibly many more than that – I'm keen to pass on some tips about working with guests.

I haven't seen any guidance on this in any of the other podcast books that I have read, so this is stuff that works from the broadcaster's handbook. I hope it will help you to define and refine your own interview technique.

There's no 'perfect' way to carry out an interview, but there are some pitfalls to avoid and also some practical tips that will make your life as a podcast show host much easier.

Interview planning

If you've never carried out an interview before, don't worry. Relax, take a breath and remember it's no different from meeting somebody in a bar and asking them interested questions about what they do.

Your interviewee is a human being, just like you, and they will be wondering what you're going to ask them. They will also look to you to convey that you know what you're doing. Even if you're a bit unsure of your equipment, don't apologise for your nerves; try and give the impression that everything is going as planned.

I also recommend practising first with somebody that you know. Get used to how you'll manage your equipment and make sure the guest is set up the way you want them. You may be recording them via Skype or Zoom, or they might be sitting opposite you in real life.

You must get used to asking for any changes that you want before the interview takes place. For instance, if somebody has a noisy pet, ask if they can be moved elsewhere. I once had to ask a guest to relocate a very lively parakeet. If the guest is sitting too far from or too close to the microphone, ask them to move. If they're tapping the table or sniffing while they're talking to you, ask them to refrain from doing that in the interview.

This might seem embarrassing to you, but you are in charge of making sure you get as good a quality recording as possible. And if you don't take care of these matters, nobody else will. Also, don't always assume you can take care of it in the edit. Aim to record guests in one take, without editing; it's a good discipline and will help you to get the audio processed more quickly. Aspire to become that 'one-take' interviewer; you'll thank your future self for it when you don't have to spend hours and hours trying to make something coherent out of a dodgy recording.

What I do suggest is that as the interviewer, you have some questions jotted down. Now, don't stick slavishly to these questions, your interview should always evolve naturally. My best tip is to listen to what your guest is saying, then take your question from what they just told you. Here are two examples:

Example 1

Guest: ... so after ten years of trying, I finally became a TV star.

Interviewer: Being on TV must have turned your life upside down – what changes did you have to make?

Example 2

Guest: ... it was the worst moment of my life.

Interviewer: How did you cope with what must have been a very dark period in your childhood?

If you listen to what the guest is saying, they will generally prompt your next question. There's nothing worse than hearing an interviewer ask a question that's already been answered; listen attentively and actively.

Sometimes, even as the interviewer, you get caught out. Perhaps the guest is harder work than you expected, sometimes they give a shorter answer than you were anticipating and they catch you on the hop, or you might just have a couple of questions that you simply mustn't forget to ask. Perhaps they were questions sent in by listeners or something similar.

It's always good to have a handful of questions jotted down, just in case.

Oh, and here's a really big tip. Always have a good idea what your first and last questions will be. The first question sets out your stall. It needs to be a strong question, but also one which allows the guest to warm up and get into their stride. Don't make it a challenging question, think of it as the interview equivalent of warm-up exercises.

Great questions to start with are:

- What got you started in XYZ?
- Why did you become a XYZ?
- Why did you get involved with XYZ

That first question should never be a yes/no type of question – note what I say about Who/What/When/Where/Why/How below. Write that first question down and lead with it, give it some thought before-hand and make it strong. This is what will either keep your listeners engaged or cause them to tune out.

The penultimate and final questions are also important. The penultimate question is your signal to the guest that you're getting ready to finish. It will include phrases like:

- Before we finish, I'd like to ask ...
- We're almost out of time now, so can I just check ...
- We've covered a lot of ground today, but before we conclude ...
- Our time is almost up now, so ...

Questions like this give your guest a cue that you're winding up the interview and they'll give you a shorter answer, which will ensure that the pace of your interview is correct; you don't generally want to finish on a massive, complicated answer. If they don't give you a shorter answer, rephrase the question and ask them to respond in a couple of sentences. When editing the audio, retain your original question, remove their long-winded answer and retain the short answer.

For podcasting purposes, your final question will

usually be something like the following:

- Where can we find out more about you?
- Just remind us when and where the event is taking place ...
- Finally, where can we get more information about the campaign/initiative/charity etc

Here's another tip if you're recording guests with a portable recording device; write down their name, title and a maximum of ten really brief questions on a small index card and just keep it close by in case you lose your way and need to refer to it. This is also a technique I use if I'm doing a talk and I'm a bit jittery about it. An index card with brief notes written on it is an unobtrusive way of carrying a lot of information in a very compact place.

This might all sound complicated but it's really not. Following this process will give you a strong beginning and a clear ending. Carry on reading and I'll give you some tips to make sure that the bit in the middle is also worth listening to as well.

Guest briefing & expectations

As a BBC journalist, I was expected to work to a series of guidelines which defined best practice and fair dealing. I still observe those principles as a podcast host, they're a good set of rules and will serve you well. This is far from an exhaustive list; I've just shared here the points that I consider to be most pertinent in the podcasting situation.

- Always deal fairly with a guest. Give them a good idea what you'll be talking about (an overview) and let them know if you're going to stray off-topic; nobody likes to feel they were misled or 'hijacked'. Outline the amount of time the interview will take up and respect their time – don't over-run.

- Don't provide a list of questions beforehand. The BBC doesn't do this on editorial grounds, but you shouldn't do it either, in order to discourage guests from writing scripts. By all means tell them the areas that you will cover, but not the precise questions.

- Be clear about recording. Tell them when you are recording the conversation and when you have stopped. If they tell you that something is off-the-record, respect that. If you caught it on tape, and they revealed something secret, in confidence, it's not appropriate to then broadcast it without permission. You might ask if they could express it in a different way on the record, but always deal honestly with guests.

- Be clear with a guest if the interview is going out live or if it is pre-recorded.

- Don't make commitments and promises to guests that you can't keep. For instance, don't promise that they'll make 100 sales if they talk to you on your show when you have no way of guaranteeing that.

- As a courtesy, pre-warn your guest if you're going to ask a question which may be on a touchy or sensitive topic.

- Avoid BS and exaggeration at all times.

By the way, the BBC Editorial Guidelines are available

online for all to see. If you're presenting a newsy or topical podcast, I'd recommend whizzing through them, you'll find some useful information in there.

Guest introductions

There's nothing more embarrassing than getting a guest's name or title wrong on live radio. As a presenter, you're in the hands of the producers. I was on the receiving end of a couple of 'stray-bullet' producers in my radio career, and I used to brace myself whenever they were putting together shows. I hasten to add, most of the radio producers I worked with were excellent, some of them I'd trust with my life, they were so thorough in their preparation.

In fact, this is such an occupational hazard in live broadcasting that I once devised a practical test when interviewing prospective new breakfast show co-presenters to see how they coped when the local bishop, who was a brilliant sport and had agreed to assist with the process, sternly informed them that they'd just got his name wrong in their introduction. It was interesting to see how the interviewees coped with that. One lady just giggled; she didn't get the job.

Why am I telling you this? Because I want you to make sure that you have your guest's name and job title correct when you introduce them on your podcast. This is one of the reasons I follow up interviews by sending a screenshot of their web page over; I don't want to find out that I made a mistake after the horse has bolted.

The best way to manage this, before the interview even begins, is to ask these questions and even record them before you start the formal interview, so you have them to refer back to. You will, of course, edit them out before the episode is released.

- *What do you prefer me to call you?* By your full name or the shortened version, perhaps even a nickname or pseudonym i.e. Pete or Peter, Jan or Janice?
- *How do you spell your name?* Don't be afraid or embarrassed to ask this, it's important that you get it right.
- *How would you prefer that I introduce you by your job title?* Don't guess or find it on the internet; if they tell you how they like to be introduced you can't go wrong.

These are just standard checks if you're a reporter – and that's what you are now if you're recording interviews, so it's important to behave like one.

Legal stuff

As the recorder and publisher of the interview, you are responsible for what is broadcast on your podcast. If the guest is being racist, homophobic, libellous, discussing a court case that is ongoing or doing anything else that is deemed illegal, you can't just hold your hands up and claim *I didn't say it.* The buck stops with you.

This won't restrict your life on an everyday basis, but I often hear people saying things on podcasts which make me wince as a journalist. They should think themselves lucky that they're not exposed to a much wider audience, because if there was a complaint, they would not have a leg to stand on.

As a general rule, if your podcast spreads positivity and good news in the world, saying nice things rather than spreading poison, you'll be on much safer territory. If you're going for edgy, political, satirical or controversial, I recommend you swot up on your broadcast law before you release your first episode.

As a radio journalist, I had to pass a law examination to demonstrate that I had a firm grasp of the potential hazards, and in hundreds and hundreds of live and pre-recorded radio shows, I never let a legal ball into the net. I remain just as vigilant as a podcaster; this legal stuff, however annoying it may seem, really matters.

Now, before we get into this section, I need to be clear about a couple of things. I am not a legal expert nor is this legal advice. The following should be taken as red flags, legal aspects which you need to be aware of. I highly recommend you do a bit of reading around these and I will place some useful links to help you to do so at PaulTeague.net/POD.

The main areas which could land you in trouble on a podcast are as follows;

- Libel
- Contempt of court
- Copyright

Your podcast will be internationally distributed, so it may not be just the laws of your land which apply. If you're aware of these key areas, and you steer clear of them, your podcast life will remain sweet. Let's drill down into them and I'll give you an idea of where you'll be navigating into choppy waters.

Libel – when you say something which defames an individual or organisation i.e. it damages a person's reputation by exposing them to hatred, contempt, shame or ridicule or causes a person to be avoided or shunned. The benchmark for this is a 'reasonable person' or 'right-thinking member of society'.

Libel damages can be huge, depending on what you've said and who you said it about. However, there are three defences against a libel claim:

- Justification i.e. it's true in substance and fact.
- Fair comment – it was a statement of opinion, based on fact and made in good faith.
- Privilege – a complex defence based on public interest, and normally (in the UK where I am based) relating to revelations in parliament, court activities, public enquiries and so on.

From your point of view, as a podcaster, justification would be your main defence. So basically, if you don't know it to be true, don't say it.

Now, there are many misconceptions about libel, one which particularly makes me cringe when I hear it being used by podcasters. Let's go through them now

- Peppering what you say with the word 'allegedly' does not give you some divine protection. This is the one that makes me cringe and shows me that the podcast presenter hasn't got a clue about the legal basics. Allegedly – when used correctly – is used in court reporting and relates to the charges that are made against an individual or individuals. Do not use it as some talisman against legal proceedings and if you are going to use it, please do your homework and deploy it correctly.
- You can always report facts. The burden of proof

will be on you to show that you can prove those facts, so you'd better be very sure before you make your claims. The BBC has legal experts available 24/7 and believe me, we used them. Any doubts at all and we ran queries by the lawyers. Now, remember, we were journalists and reporters, it was our job to be doing this stuff, it's what we were trained for. I'd suggest to you that you take great care and get yourself a qualification in journalism if you intend to stray into this potentially hazardous territory.

- You can't repeat a libellous comment just because somebody else made it. It's just as libellous and you're spreading it even further. In this scenario, you will both be held to account.
- A claim might still be libellous, even if it is reported as a rumour and even if it is reported as being untrue. Remember those tests – hatred, contempt, shame or ridicule etc – they might still apply if you share something horrible about somebody, you state it to be untrue, but you spread the malice anyway.
- A comment may be libellous even if the person is sitting directly in front of you and they have the right of reply.
- Generalising from specific and true allegations may well be libellous. If somebody has previously been convicted for theft, you can't then claim that they're probably responsible for some other incident just because they have previous 'form'.
- You can libel somebody without naming them. In contempt of court (below) this is like the

jigsaw effect, when we all know who you're talking about from the snippets you've given us, even if you don't name them.

- Context counts! If you're hosting a satirical comedy show, you're much more likely to get away with something than if you're a reporter on a news show. However, if you do sail close to the wind, know your law. All those panel shows that you watch on the BBC are monitored by BBC lawyers – just in case.

Contempt of court – this relates to what you may – and may not say about a trial. It's based on the concept of being innocent until proven guilty. In the UK we're entitled to a fair trial, and to be judged by a jury made up of our peers. While the case is active, you are not allowed to conjecture or theorise about whether the accused is guilty or not, nor reveal information which may sway jurors. You can't say things like: *He's probably guilty* or *I reckon she did it* because this is contempt of court. Neither can you describe the accused in court in emotive terms, such as: *He sat in the dock with a violent, sneering look.*

In a famed UK incident, two presenters were removed from their jobs because of making comments just like these in a high-profile and very emotive trial. This one is really important and can land you in big trouble. I was once involved in a court request for audio from one of my radio shows because there had been a suggestion that there was an issue. The request came through the judge. It's a bit stressful when it happens, but we were fine, as we knew we most likely were.

Contempt of Court in the UK is a criminal rather than a

civil matter, which means you might go to jail for it. If not, you'll get a fine.

Social media is particularly susceptible to this 'trial by mob' syndrome and people forget that when they write something on social media – just as when you release a podcast episode – you become a broadcaster with the same legal obligations and penalties as a national newspaper or household name broadcaster.

The only safe approach – as with libel – is to be extremely cautious. In all my dealings on social media and on my podcast, I follow the sound advice of Thumper the rabbit in the Disney cartoon. To paraphrase that wise rabbit, if you haven't got anything good to say, you're generally best not saying anything at all.

Copyright - copyright law will vary depending upon where you live in the world, but I can give you some general rules of thumb. Just because you found it on the internet, doesn't mean you can help yourself to it without permission. That includes photos, music, audio, artwork, videos, quotations … if somebody else originated it, you'd better be darn sure you have explicit permission to use it before you help yourself. Don't risk it if you think you might get away with it; you'll be building your business on sand if you do.

There are some exemptions with copyright law – such as fair use – but my personal policy is to avoid at all costs.

What does this mean for podcasters?

- Make sure you have the rights to use music in your show. There are web services dedicated specifically to this purpose, and I will share some favourites at PaulTeague.net/POD.
- Ensure that you use licenced imagery for your show. I recommend using Canva for all your

graphics work, it'll keep you straight from a copyright point of view and won't cost the earth.

- If you get a logo designed, make sure you use a service which only uses licensed imagery. If you're not sure, check.
- Don't play-in film or TV clips, read extracts from books or poems or share extracts from your favourite bands or artists. Not even a tiny bit – ever.

You may accuse me of spoiling all your fun. I'm trying to help you to avoid a big fine. Don't even risk it, remain compliant at all times.

When I worked at the BBC, I was offered a pre-recorded programme which featured poetry readings from a nationally known poet. I was assured that the poet herself had given permission for the freelancer to use the poems. Only, under copyright law, it wasn't up to the poet to give that permission. The copyright was owned by the poet's publisher and they knew nothing about the programme. It turns out that a one-hour programme which was being sold to us for no more than two hundred pounds was going to cost several times that if we even used a fraction of the poetry readings that it included. Phew! Bullet well-and-truly-dodged.

The moral of all this? Always, always check the licence. There are plenty of websites available to sell you correctly licensed images and music; use them and make sure you study their licence details to ensure you are working within their rules.

And a final reminder. I am not a legal expert nor is this legal advice. Check the rules in the country in which you're based. You're the host of the show, you're in charge and it's your responsibility. And no, you can't blame me.

Podcast release forms

Opinions vary greatly about whether you need these or not. The basic premise is that you get podcast guests to sign a legal form which sets out your rights and their rights in very specific terms. I have never used these, though you will note that every podcast guest on my show is sent the link to my FAQs page where I outline the same sort of information that you would find in a release form.

Now, I am not a legal expert, and this is not legal advice (did I mention that already?). However, my feeling is that most of the guests I have spoken to would run a mile at the prospect of having to wade through and sign a form that's packed with legal jargon, so my choice was to avoid it. However, I do understand that, strictly speaking, it's a good and sensible thing to do.

I recommend doing a web search for *podcast release form* so that you can see what's involved. There are even templates which are offered free of charge online – and you'll have to make up your own mind about this one. Gordon Firemark is the best source of targeted information I have found on this topic and I highly recommend you searching out his excellent content online and learning from a legal expert.

Asking good questions

The best kind of questions to ask are open questions i.e. questions which lead somewhere. A question like *What's your favourite colour?* takes us nowhere that's useful. A question like *What's your favourite colour and why is that?* won't win any journalism awards, but it will get the guest talking. The best questions start with the following words:

- Who?
- What?
- When?
- Where?
- Why?
- How?

If you ask questions which inspire one-word answers, you'll have to work really hard as an interviewer If you want to enjoy somebody else's discomfort, watch how most reporters struggle when speaking to children. Most kids don't develop their answers, and caught on the back foot, interviewers end up asking rapid-fire questions which only get returned with one-word answers. And yes, I have been there. It's really difficult interviewing kids. Occasionally they create radio magic; most times it's hard work.

Overcomplicated questions

I was listening to a podcast the other day where the presenter's questions were so long and convoluted, I was completely confused about the question that was being asked. There were so many diversions and circumlocutions, if I had been the guest on the receiving end, I'd have had to ask her to express her point in a single sentence. I suspect this was caused by lack of preparation. Waffling is a diversionary tactic used by presenters who haven't got a clue what they want to ask next. This lady was thrashing around until she found her question among all the chaff. By the way, I really like this lady, her topic and her show, but she was driving me mad with her questions.

Please keep your questions to the point and clear. I listen to experienced presenters on the BBC's Today programme almost every morning saying things like *In a word, please would you explain XYZ* then they take about two minutes to ask some ridiculous, convoluted sub-question. I prefer the 1-2 question technique. Refer to what they've been saying (show you're listening) then ask a clear and pertinent question which moves it forward. If you need to change the subject, use a simple bridging sentence like: *I want to talk about your life as a teenager now* ... then ask your question. Don't ask several questions, make it clear and concise. And make sure there's a question in there; sometimes I hear presenters make a statement and there's no actual question in there.

This makes life easier for your interviewee too; give them a fighting chance by at least offering some clarity.

Remember at all times that the interview is about your guest – not you – so we generally want to be hearing their voice much more than yours.

A way to inoculate yourself against rambling until you think of a question is to have that list of prompts handy. If you get caught on the hop, it's always there, ready to serve as a safety net whenever you need it.

Podcast introductions

I'm a fan of getting to the point fast when I'm releasing interview episodes of my podcast. I don't like a lot of messing around; my policy is to introduce the guest and get them sharing juicy morsels of information as soon as possible.

Remember, when you release guest episodes, it's all about them, not you.

You can cover a lot of the essential information in a tightly-written introduction, we call it a cue in radio. I present my guest shows in exactly the same way as I did pre-recorded interviews for the radio, only they're longer, of course.

I've given two examples below of interview scripts which I used for real on my Self-Publishing Journeys podcast. Note the following about both of these cues:

- Each episode is anchored by date and show number for easy identification and sequencing.
- I cover the basics about each author – the list of facts – so that we can get on with the interesting stuff straight away. I've removed the need for them to tell me this basic info.
- I edit out my first question of the recording – missing the: *Hello, how are you?* bits and even my first question so that the guest starts strong and confident on their first answer ... more on this when I talk about editing later.
- Each interview has what we referred to in radio as a 'back anno' – a back announcement – which is basically to reiterate who the guest was and to trail ahead (or promote) the next podcast episode.

Guest example script 1

Hello and welcome to SPJ Episode 115, for Monday 14th May 2018.

My guest today is Clare Sager, a lifelong fantasy reader, former English teacher, and corsetière.

Her fate was set the day her father gave her a DragonLance graphic novel – after that, there was no hope for her to be anything other than a speculative fiction author.

When she's not writing, she can be found reading, role-playing, gaming, or laughing at cats/photos of cats.

She lives in Nottingham, Robin Hood country, so it's no surprise she writes about a character who robs from the rich to give to the poor.

Clare has been a long-time listener to this podcast and has posted several images to Twitter showing the progress of her wedding dress as she catches up with weekly episodes.

When we spoke for the podcast, I started by asking her what that first book - DragonLance - sparked off in her from a creative point of view ...

Thanks for listening to this week's interview ... I'll have another edition of Paul's podcast diary for you on Saturday and my next author interview will be dropped into the podcast feed on Monday 4th June, when I'll be chatting to physics textbook writer and self-published whodunnit and sci-fi author Miles Hudson.

Miles managed to fully fund his sci-fi novel on Unbound, so among other things, we'll be chatting about how he did that.

Until next time, have a great week of writing, bye for now!

Guest example script 2

Welcome to SPJ episode 117 for Monday 18th June 2018.
Miles Hudson was a secondary school physics teacher for more
than 20 years and has been writing physics textbooks for more
than 15 years.

He also invented - and now sells from his website - the Best Fit
Line Ruler which he created for science and maths education.

By his own admission, textbook writing is quite uninspiring
work, so Miles also writes fiction to feed his creativity.

His first novel was a whodunit, The Cricketer's Corpse, but his
latest story - 2089 - is much more of a real piece of literature and
was crowdfunded via Unbound.

I met Miles through a digital project which was being run by
New Writing North and we worked together on the project
between April and May.

When we chatted for the podcast, I started by asking Miles how
he got involved with writing textbooks as a teacher ...

Thanks for listening to this week's interview ... I'll have another
edition of Paul's podcast diary for you on Saturday and my next
author interview will be dropped into the podcast feed on
Monday 25th June, when I'll be chatting to multi-award-winning
Scottish author, screenwriter and writer of comics, Barry Hutchi-

son, with over 80 trade-published children's books to his credit, who turned indie in 2016 after ten years of being trade-published – and he is very glad he did!

Until next time, have a great week of writing, bye for now!

I used to record those introductions while the guest was waiting for me on Skype, but I stopped that sharpish to spare them the pain of when I messed it up and had to start again to get a good take recorded. I prefer instead to have the pre-chat, tell them I've started recording, then asking them my first question. I've had listeners tell me they like the way I just get on with my interviews with all the pleasantries and superfluous stuff edited out. It's always up to you how you run your show, of course, but that's how we did it when I was at the BBC.

Interruptions

Sometimes it's necessary to interrupt a guest. It may be on a simple point – maybe they've used a term or referred to something you don't understand and you need a clarification – it might even be because their answer is dragging on a bit and you need to chivvy them along. As the person in charge of the interview, sometimes you need to interrupt and, so long as you don't do it for the sake of it, you should deploy this tactic if necessary.

It's up to you to steer and control each interview, to make the guest sound as good as they can and to extract great information for your listeners. Like the sailor with their hand on the tiller, you need to make sure your interview is a safe journey from A-to-Z and that it comes into the marina nice and steady with a great conclusion and ending. Sometimes guests need a little prod; that's your job, just in case you weren't already aware of that.

Messing up

I mess up all the time. I know the rules, I know what's supposed to be best practice and still I mess up. We're human beings; sometimes our mouths won't do what we want, sometimes our brains won't do what we want and sometimes neither of them will do what we want. Don't beat yourself up about it. Eventually you'll be able to let a robot present your show and then it will be error free but completely bland and monotonous; which would you prefer?

The simple truth that I learnt on the radio is that the best presenters are usually those who throw out the rule book and just come over as regular human beings. They're always the most popular presenters too. It's why you should always be yourself; that's what listeners will like about you.

Because I've presented so many hours of live radio, I tend to treat my podcast recordings that way too. I simply don't have the time to spend four hours or more editing each episode, so listeners have to take it warts and all. The alternative is that I wouldn't have time to get the episodes out. That means there are more ums and ahs than I'd like, but I'm busking it, working from a set of bullet points, that's how it has to be.

I generally work through my mess-ups and laugh them off or just work around them. Try to get used to recording your show 'as-live', that is, as if you were streaming it live on Facebook or YouTube and you just had to keep going, what-ever happened. It's a good discipline and will help you reduce editing time when you build up your confidence.

Paying an audio editor

You can always employ an audio editor to take care of your episodes. This will be a more expensive option – you have been warned – and you will also get what you pay for.

Always ask for an edited sample before commissioning an audio editor. Also, allow a 1:4 ratio for editing time. That means you should expect to pay for four hours of editing for every hour of audio. It takes time to do it properly – you wouldn't be outsourcing the job if it didn't – which is why I recommend a one-take strategy; try to get used to recording shows in a single take so they only require minimal editing work.

Editing tips

Editing is a bit of an art form, and it's something that I could do all day long if I had the time. The sheer joy of making an edit which you can't detect when you listen back to the audio is indescribable. You're unlikely to be a brilliant editor from the get-go, but as you edit more and more audio, you'll speed up and your judgement about what gets edited and what does not will become more assured.

Although it's impossible to teach you how to edit in a book, I can give you a number of practical tips which will set you on the right path.

Beware of over-editing

A lot of podcasters edit their audio within an inch of its life. They remove every single um and ah, even breaths. Now let me set out my stall with that; it's ridiculous and I don't want you to do it. I am a big believer in the natural rhythms of speech. In real conversations people pause, consider, get their words wrong, um and ah. If you remove all of those things in an edit, you will make you and your guest sound like automatons. It sounds unnatural and ridiculous.

I mentioned earlier in the book the podcast which I really want to listen to, but it's been edited in this manner. I can't keep up with it, it's just too intense, I need the natural spaces and pace of a conversation to be able to retain it.

My advice to you is to remove the worst of it, if it's even there in the first place, but to ensure at all times that those natural rhythms of speech are retained, out of consideration for the listener. Even on the radio we didn't edit those things out; we didn't have time and it sounded terrible if we did. Don't over-edit. Trim it up, enhance it so the annoying bits are removed, make the guest sound good, but if we wanted to listen to robots presenting a show, we'd get Alexa to read out the alphabet to us.

Get used to 'topping and tailing' your recordings

You should aim to get your recordings so that you can remove the shuffling, coughing and pre-amble at the beginning, and the fumbling for the stop button at the end, and very quickly isolate the core audio which will form the podcast episode. This is called *topping and tailing* in the industry; in layman's terms it means cutting off the rubbish at the beginning and the end. That's your first job after making sure your audio is saved; to isolate the core audio which you need to work on.

When I get a recording in one take, I top and tail it, process it in Libsyn, and off we go, it's ready to release. It's always good to aspire to be able to do this, you'll thank yourself for it when you're tight on time and you need to get that week's episode out fast.

Use the three-clap technique if you make a mess-up

If you make a serious mess up – one which will have to be edited out – here's a ninja tip for you. Pause a moment, then clap three times, sharp and crisp. Pause again, then carry on speaking. When it comes to the edit, those three claps will be easy to spot, they appear as three tall peaks in the audio editing display. That will help you to find where the edit is faster and mean that you can get your audio processed and published sooner.

If you do mess up, I recommend starting your last sentence again, so that you can get a nice, clean edit point. Always leave a pause beforehand, it will make it much easier to make a seamless edit.

In summary, some mess ups you should laugh about and carry on, others will need to be edited. I tend to edit out coughs, splutters and pauses to drink my cup of tea. I'll only edit a speech mess up if I was unable to recover from it and it was necessary to start again.

Take care when editing breaths

We all have to breathe. I know I'm stating the obvious, but it needs to be said. That's why I can't understand why some podcast hosts edit out the breaths, to me it seems a ridiculous notion. The breaths are important, they help to preserve the natural rhythms of speech which, as you know by now, I firmly believe in. But as well as leaving breaths in when you edit, I want you to take particular care what you do with them when you're editing a piece of audio. Sometimes you'll hear a really sharp edit, where the voice of the audio seems to move between words in an impossibly quick time. That usually means a breath was removed. And sometimes you'll hear two breaths in a row, where somebody made an edit and paid no attention to that phrase I love so much – the natural rhythms of speech. Breaths can be your friend in an edit, making the transition from one editing point to another seamless.

If I have to edit two sentences – or parts of sentences – I tend to preserve the breath from the first sentence, remove it from the second, and join the two parts together. If that doesn't work, I try it the other way around, removing the breath from the first part of the audio and leaving it in the second. You'll generally find you get a clean edit that way and that the seam can't be heard when you listen back

Don't get hung up with the editing

I know I sound gung-ho about a lot of this stuff, but I've edited thousands of hours of audio, often at great speed, and you acquire a pretty good idea about what can stay in a recording and what has to go after you've been doing it for a while. I have a good sense of what's a deal-breaker and what can stay in a piece of audio, particularly if I'm working under tight time constraints. Let's face it, when aren't we working against the clock?

For that reason, I don't want you to get hung up about editing. I learnt a very important lesson about this early on, before I was even employed by the BBC. I had popped into my local radio station in my home town – here's a shout-out for the fabulous BBC Radio Lincolnshire – and I had managed to sweet-talk the news team into letting a complete rookie go out onto the streets with a UHER reel-to-reel recorder to get some vox pops about the New Year UK sales.

I'd managed to get some audio recorded, and I was editing the tape – if you're younger than twenty, you'll have to look it up in the history books if you don't know what tape is. In those days – and no laughing please – we used to mark the tape with a white, chinagraph pencil and cut it diagonally with a razor blade. I'll give the youngsters reading five minutes to stop laughing. I know, it's positively primitive, but that's how it was done for years. I had gone through the tape, cutting out all the separate clips of speech that I wanted to use in my vox pop, and I had about twenty lengths of tape hanging around my neck. I was agonising about which order to assemble them in and I'd over-recorded, so some I'd have to leave out.

The presenter walked by – on his way to go live on air in the studios – and asked me how I was getting on and if it would be ready in time. That's all he cared about, and for good reason. If I didn't deliver, he had a gap in his show.

He gave me great advice and I remember it, and act upon it, to this day.

If you're not ready for your slot on time, nobody will ever hear what you recorded. Nobody knows or cares what ended up in the bin; choose four - five decent sections of tape for the vox pop, stick them together with editing tape, and get it out on time.

I'll just give the youngsters reading another five minutes to laugh about us having to stick the piece of recording tape together with splicing tape. Yup, I really am that old. But that presenter was absolutely right. People only judge you on what they get to hear. They never know what got edited out. And if you don't get it out on time, they'll never hear it anyway.

Please stop paralysing yourself with indecision, make

those swift and confident editing decisions and let's get those podcast episodes released on time.

Remove anything that concerns you

You are the final gatekeeper of your show, the buck stops with you. If the guest says anything offensive, off-colour, legally dubious or lacking in substance or truth, edit it out. Just edit out your question and their answer and move onto the next bit. You are the editor; you are responsible for making sure that each episode is fit to air when it's released.

A judge won't care if you use the excuse, *I thought it was alright as the guest said it, not me.* You are the publisher and it's up to you to remove it in the edit.

Most of the time, this won't be a problem. Just use a bit of common sense and judgement. But if something doesn't sit right with you, if you're wondering if it might come over as offensive, I'd always err on the side of caution and edit it out. You'll never get into trouble for something that didn't appear in the show – nobody even knows it was supposed to be there in the first place – but you may well get into trouble for something which you didn't edit out. If you use the FAQ text that I shared with you earlier – or adapt it for your own purposes – that makes it completely clear to prospective guests that you reserve the right to edit as you see fit.

Don't ever feel like you need to be defensive about your editorial judgements, create a show you can be proud and confident of.

Tedious bits of housekeeping

Most shows have their tedious bits. By this, I mean house-keeping tasks such as welcoming new Patreon supporters, announcing competition winners, stuff like that. Here's my tip for that; don't put your tedious stuff at the beginning of the show.

There's one show I listen to – and really like, I hasten to add – where we have to go through about twelve minutes of housekeeping tedium before we get to the stuff I tuned in for. I simply don't care, if I didn't know the good stuff was on its way, I'd switch off. Here's a radical suggestion for you; leave the boring stuff until the end. I'm a big fan of getting on with business, I have a low tolerance level for pleasantries and superfluous stuff. I know these tasks need to be done, but please park them at the end so we can tune out if we don't want to hear them. As a former radio show presenter, it seems crazy to me that you'd saddle your show with boring bits at the beginning; at the very least they should be sandwiched somewhere in the middle. So please think of it from a showbiz point of view and be considerate of your listeners at all times.

Things that you must always edit out

- Coughs, splutters and burps.
- Expletives (unless you intend to add an Advisory tag when you list your show).
- Incessantly noisy animals or children.
- Mistakes that are just plain embarrassing.
- Offensive comments.
- Excessive ums and ahs ... if you're listening to audio and you're thinking 'just get on with it' that suggests it's time for an edit.

Key points

- Plan your interviews but don't script them. Listen to your guests and be attentive to what they say.
- Learn interviewing best practice techniques and always deal with guests in a professional and organised way.
- Don't forget your legal obligations as a podcaster. Be aware of the potential pitfalls before you get started.

11

ACCELERATE YOUR PODCAST

This is where we go pro – but only if you want to. I've recommended so far that you set up a simple podcast – nothing too fancy – and that it's not over-ambitious in terms of what you're reaching for. Once you've got those first ten episodes released, this is what happens next.

I want you to record, edit, publish and release your first ten episodes before you even consider my ideas below. If you've done that and you still feel enthusiastic and full of beans, you'll be ready to push the boat out a little further.

Musical inserts & voiceovers

I recommended that you start off without music beds and fancy jingles. However, this is a good thing to be working on once the show is going. There are many ways to achieve this task, and I'd generally recommend that you outsource the job unless you know what you're doing with audio mixing.

I get my jingle vocals recorded on Fiverr.com and my music from premiumbeat.com. There are other services available and I'll share some of these over at Paul-Teague.net/POD. You'll find audio editors on sites like Fiverr, Elance and People Per Hour. If you want to have a go yourself, that's also fine, just remember the following rules of mixing music and speech;

- The speech must be more dominant than the music.
- At the point where the audio insert comes in, drop the level of the music on a beat or at an appropriate point so that it doesn't sound grating on the ear.
- Fade music out or use a track which has a proper ending – a 'hard ending' as we used to refer to it in radio.
- Use licensed music at all times.

Better podcast kit

Up until this point, you may have used the basic Logitech headset that I recommended or perhaps even a microphone that you owned already. After getting ten episodes in the pot, you might now wish to get something a bit better, a microphone which is higher quality.

At this stage, with ten episodes behind you, we're out of the *all-the-gear-and-no-idea* zone, so I'm now happy for you to spend a bit of cash if your budget allows. I'm going to remind you that the best sources of great information here – without you ending up with a million-pound recording studio that would impress even The Rolling Stones – are UK podcast expert, Colin Gray and US podcasting veteran, David Jackson. These guys have all the knowledge and experience in this area and get my thumbs up because they also take account of practicalities and budgets. They'll be able to give you a range of options to suit all spending levels.

Good reviews – bad reviews

You're going to start getting reviews on your podcast and most of the time these will be positive and ego-boosting. Celebrate that, you know you're doing something right.

However, every now and then, you might get a negative review and they can sting when they arrive. Here's a bit of guidance when those much-wanted reviews start to arrive:

- Never berate a person for leaving a bad review. They can be infuriating, frustrating, demoralising and just plain wrong. But we have to wear our big boy/girl pants and take it on the chin; it comes with the territory.
- If a negative review is libellous, racist, homophobic or anything else that causes concern, every podcast channel has a button which will allow you to report abuse. Only use this functionality if it genuinely is abuse of the system, don't use it just because you don't like a review.
- Print out your positive reviews and stick them on the wall. If ever you're feeling demoralised by someone's negativity, sit back and admire those great reviews and take consolation that while they're spreading vitriol, you're sending great things out into the world.

Monetising with Patreon

It seems like every podcaster these days is using Patreon to encourage financial support for their show and I will admit that I have dabbled with Patreon too. Patreon allows your listeners to give you financial support at different levels, usually based on tiered incentives or extra content.

There's absolutely no reason why you shouldn't dabble with Patreon on a *nothing ventured, nothing gained* basis, but I do have some thoughts to share with you before going down this route:

- Having used Patreon myself, I think it will feel like you're flogging a dead horse if you don't have *a lot* of listeners. I sometimes hear podcast presenters working so hard to encourage Patreon supporters, it makes me feel tired just hearing about all the extra work they're doing. I would tend to hold back on Patreon until you build a keen and motivated core of listeners.
- When I tried to get my Patreon channel going, it became one more thing to put my already limited amount of time under considerable pressure. I was getting a reasonable amount of Patreon support – enough to make it financially worthwhile – but not so much that it justified all the time it took me to feed that extra content requirement.
- If you listen to a lot of podcasts, it gets a bit wearing hearing virtually every podcast host thrashing their Patreon channel. A PayPal donate button does pretty well the same thing, you don't have to use Patreon.

- Don't announce that you have no new Patreon supporters on your podcast, it doesn't make it sound like a very enticing prospect. Instead, encourage listeners to join all the other Patreon supporters who are already enjoying exclusive benefits and VIP access. Make it sound exciting; sometimes I just want to shed a tear when presenters get no new supporters week after week. Don't tell me that, I don't need to know it. This is showbiz.

To transcribe or not to transcribe?

You may have noticed that many podcasters transcribe their shows and wondered why they do this. There are two main reasons; the first is that it helps with SEO – Search Engine Optimisation; the other is that it provides a useful service to podcast consumers, many of whom will prefer to absorb information in a text format. And in case you've never heard of transcribing before, it's where your audio is taken and then typed out as text, much like the script of a play, with speakers indicated where there is more than one voice.

Let's take the first of those uses – SEO. One of the fabulous things about a podcast interview is that it is packed with keywords related to your theme or niche. Google loves keywords; they serve as an indicator as to what a piece of content is about, thus allowing the search engine to deliver relevant results. If you add your episode transcription to your show notes, over time you build up a rich reservoir of keyworded articles which, in turn, help your blog or website get discovered in the search engines.

Now, there are a couple of flags to raise here. As we increasingly become more dependent upon services such as

Siri, Google Assistant and Alexa, voice-based services will begin to dominate over text. Online videos are already being subtitled automatically and audio will likely follow, give or take the odd legal challenge here and there over intellectual property. It may come to pass that keywording via on-page text becomes less important over time, in which case you may decide not to bother.

Transcription by humans can be very expensive. Transcription by artificial intelligence is cheaper, but extremely unreliable. I've tried both, I prefer transcription by humans at the time of writing. Other than testing the water, I have never bothered to get my interviews transcribed – and if I did, I would probably approach the matter strategically, waiting until I had some statistics showing me which of my episodes were most popular, then paying to get them transcribed. I believe that subtitling of audio or very cheap and accurate transcription by AI is not far off; this may be the best cost vs. accuracy approach to the issue.

I would advise that transcription is simply too expensive to commit to in the early days of a podcast and I'd recommend tucking it up your sleeve for later. In four years of releasing shows I have never taken a query on this issue from a listener asking why no transcription is available.

The second reason for using transcriptions is to provide a service for consumers of your show. Some people prefer to listen, others like to watch, many like to read. My compromise here is to provide web-based show notes with the crucial website links and talking points referenced. Once again, I'll remind you that I have never been asked for transcriptions for my shows, so I view them as 'nice to have' rather than essential. My recommendation is that you adopt a bootstrapping strategy as far as transcriptions are concerned; if you can't fund them from income derived directly from your podcast, the reality is that you probably don't have enough listeners yet for this issue to even make much of a difference.

Unsolicited pitches

One of the annoying things that will happen the moment you create a podcast which people can find online is that you will get unsolicited pitches. Most of these will be of the 'I have a fascinating guest who will be a great fit for your show' variety, and when you read their profile you'll wonder if they even bothered listening to your show before they reached out to you.

As a newbie podcast show host, you may well be flattered by this at first; don't be, it's a type of promotional spam and will take up – and waste – a lot of your time if you're not careful. Here's how I suggest dealing with this:

- Publish a guest/interview policy page and place it somewhere prominent on your website. Be clear about your policy: *Please do not send unsolicited guest pitches* is pretty clear, I'd say.
- This will not stop the unsolicited pitches coming. Have a standard, one-sentence reply ready to hand: *Please note that this podcast does not accept unsolicited pitches. Please read our guest policy for more information [insert web link here]*. You even get to sneak in a passive-aggressive comment reminding them that if they'd taken two minutes to do their homework, they would have realised that already.

Many people who are 'doing the rounds' on podcasts get their assistants to contact everybody and anybody to try and land them a guest slot. As far as I'm concerned, it's really rude not to check out somebody's show properly beforehand, prior to making one of these pitches. The only time I relented on my policy – against my better judgement – I got my first ever and only no-show guest to date. When I pre-vet guests and make my own decisions as to who will make a good fit, I get none of these problems.

Affiliate marketing

Affiliate marketing is a thing of great beauty and I recommend you acquaint yourself with its principles before you move on to services like Patreon or show sponsorships. I began my working life online as an affiliate marketer and I have generated thousands of dollars from deploying this marketing technique. However, a word of context before you get carried away with the excitement of it all; the majority of those thousands of dollars were earned whilst working as an internet marketer, alongside a whole bunch of ninja marketing strategies. Fewer dollars than I'd like were earned as a by-product of podcasting.

What is affiliate marketing? When you become an affiliate for a product or service, you receive a commission for recommending it, at no extra cost to the purchaser. Think of it like a referral fee. Not every product or service has a referral programme and some commissions paid are so low they're barely worth bothering with.

Amazon is usually a good fit for most podcasters, seeing as Jeff Bezos and his team seem to sell pretty well every item there is on earth these days. If you join the Amazon

Associates programme, you receive a very small commission during a specified time period, at the time of writing it's up to 12%. Now, if somebody clicks your Amazon referral link and goes on to buy a flat screen TV within the referral window, that's a decent commission. The gritty reality of Amazon affiliate income is that most people won't be buying items of that size and price and most of your monthly commissions will be low, unless you have a large audience, sufficient to generate a lot of affiliate weblink clicks.

However, I'm not trying to encourage you away from affiliate marketing, I'd just advise setting reasonable expectations around the level of income that can be generated from a podcast with a relatively small audience. With that said, here are my affiliate marketing tips:

- Never become an affiliate for products that you haven't used; it's best to select services which you know, like and use, and can recommend with a clear conscience. Your reputation is at stake here, take care with what you recommend.
- Not all products and services have affiliate programmes.
- I have found that it works best as a podcast host to seek out the affiliate programmes for all of the products I use in my business. That way, as I mention them each week, I can add my affiliate links to the show notes and encourage listeners to purchase those items via my commission-earning weblinks.
- Always be very clear if you're using an affiliate weblink, don't deceive your listeners.
- Note that most affiliate programmes will insist

that you have some form of disclaimer on your website – always read the small print or else you may find your commissions withheld or confiscated.

- Most affiliate programmes have terms and conditions attached. Amazon, by way of example, will only allow you to use their weblinks in certain circumstances. Always read the T&Cs – however boring – and don't break the rules. If you do, you may find that commissions are withheld temporarily or permanently, and you could even find yourself removed as an affiliate.

I'm a big fan of affiliate marketing (done well) for podcasters, because there will be many products and services that are a good fit for your topic and niche and – so long as you're only recommending the good stuff – it provides a useful and valuable service to your listeners if you share great tools. Never be tempted by greed to recommend useless, shoddy or irrelevant items however, or it will soon come back and bite you by diminishing your excellent reputation. The best policy with affiliate marketing is simple: integrity at all times.

Taking adverts and sponsorships

Much of what I have said about affiliate marketing applies to sponsorship of your podcast. Sponsorship is very often seen as the Holy Grail for podcasters, but it should be used with caution as with all commercial elements which you add to your show.

Podcast sponsorship takes a variety of forms and usually

involves payment based upon the number of downloads your show gets. That isn't always the case, but it is the norm. If you barely have any downloads, you're unlikely to have offers of sponsorship rolling in. However, low listener figures and sponsorship deals aren't mutually exclusive. A very niche, high-quality podcast might deliver such a good-fit audience for a product or service that you may prove irresistible to a sponsor.

My advice with sponsorship is to take note as a listener as to what works well and what doesn't. My personal opinion is that the best sponsorship has a strong affinity with the show's content; as a listener, I don't like irrelevant adverts, they spoil my enjoyment of a podcast.

Joanna Penn of The Creative Penn is my personal favourite example of sponsorship done well. She only connects with sponsors whose services she uses and loves, and she never runs adverts which seem disjointed from her podcast content. She either gets the service providers to record bespoke promotional content for her show or she reads the promo script herself, explaining how she uses the services in her own business. The way Joanna incorporates sponsors makes them an integral part of the show, a genuine partner and an excellent fit for the rest of her podcast's content.

This speaks once again to the need for integrity in what you're promoting. As a podcast host your integrity and trustworthiness is paramount; never sacrifice these in your search for a quick buck. One of the unseen benefits of becoming a podcast host is that you will be seen by your listeners as a trusted guide and reliable source of information. It's a good idea not to squander that position.

Many podcasting services deliver adverts via a feed and

you have no – or very little control – over what is delivered to your show using this technique. You may be tempted at first to try to squeeze any money out of your show, however paltry the takings. I would always caution hanging on for the right partnership; if you get it wrong you can very easily dilute your strong, well-defined brand. This is why I encourage new podcasters not to bet the farm when they begin their broadcasting journey; keep your costs low, maintain a lean business in the early days, and that way you can hold out for the right type of sponsorship. However tempting random ad feeds may seem as a road to easy income, they're likely to put off many listeners and some will even switch away.

Another thing you have to be careful of is being driven by the number of downloads on your show. Now there's no doubt that this is the metric that excites advertisers – and it certainly serves as an excellent bargaining chip if you're ever lucky enough to get caught up in a bidding war – but I'd always encourage making sponsorship decisions based on editorial judgements rather than marketing metrics. You'd expect me to say that as a former BBC man, so I'm not going to disappoint; I've said it anyway.

Training & advisory services

My favourite way of monetising a podcast because it plays to all the strengths of affiliate marketing and sponsorship deals without the potential negatives, is to create your own products and services around the theme of your show and to make these available to your listeners.

Your show listeners love you already; they'd be long gone if they didn't. Which means you already have one of the essential components of successful sales, the sometimes elusive *know, like and trust* factor. Your show listeners hear you every week, they feel like they know you already, they wouldn't listen if they didn't like you and the trust factor is something that you earn over time. It makes all the sense in the world for you to create your own products and services so that listeners can access the expertise and experience which you already share with them for free in every episode of your show. I call this *expert positioning*.

Here's a list of some products and services you could build around your show:

- A paid, online course, delivered via Teachable and recorded in Camtasia.
- An ebook and paperback, sold on Amazon, sharing your best tips learnt or shared on the show.
- A mastermind group, bringing together the most motivated people in your listener group.
- An in-person, paid event, bringing together fans of the show for a day/weekend of learning and networking.
- Paid 'how-to' webinars covering different elements of your niche area.

If you have the skills and drive to pursue this strategy, it can be extremely effective. As an affiliate, you only get the crumbs at the table; as the product creator, you get to eat the feast. If you take sponsorship, a third party gets the benefit of the audience you've built up around you; if you promote and sell your own products, not only is it a great fit for your show and totally 'on brand', you already have a group of pre-sold customers who are already consuming and loving your content.

Here's a tip though: it's always best to make the first product a low barrier to entry, such as an ebook or a paperback. At the back of the book, have a link to your Teachable course, moving up the price a notch. At the end of your Teachable course, have a link to your mastermind group (up goes the price tag) and then your personal, 1-1 consultancy (and up goes the price again).

This is known as a product escalator, it's the online equivalent of not asking somebody to marry you on the first date. Make your first sale item a low-price, low-risk item, move your prospects up each step of the escalator, increasing the commitment in steps. The people who work with you in mastermind groups will be your best, most committed listeners, because they recognise the value of your expertise and they're happy to pay for it. You'll enjoy working with them much more too.

As a recovering internet marketer, this is by far my preferred option for monetising podcasts; it's a really good fit for the format and works extremely well with the expert positioning model.

As you might expect, I have written a book about this very topic. You can find out more about it at PaulTeague.net/DIGITAL.

Key points

- As your podcast matures, it's likely that you'll want to start looking at ways of generating an income from your show and perhaps even spending some money on making it more professional.

- I'm not a fan of Patreon (unless you have a large, active audience), sponsorship or transcripts.
- The best and most profitable way to make money from your podcast is by creating your own products. This includes books, training courses, live events, mastermind groups and webinars.

12

GROWING YOUR PODCAST AUDIENCE

It's one thing to get your podcast launched and 'out there', it's another thing altogether for prospective listeners to find it and to start building that audience of loyal fans. There is a misconception with anything online that if you build something the customers will immediately follow. That is not always the case, and it was my first hard lesson to learn when I began to work with websites. You need to build up web traffic for your online venture in order to grow your audience and that will require you to learn some basic tricks about marketing.

Many people shudder when they hear the word *marketing*, as it conjures up images of sleazy salespeople peddling their wares. It needn't be like that, of course, and I would prefer you think of podcast promotion like a matchmaking website, only we're introducing listeners to your show, it costs nothing and it may well enhance their life or knowledge as a consequence of discovering you. There's nothing to lose here, after all your online show is a free service and nobody is forced to listen if they're really not interested.

It's important to remember that as most podcasts don't make money – particularly at the beginning – I would caution against spending advertising money to get the word out. My rule of thumb with advertising is that I only pay for it if I have a way of making that expenditure back. If I can't earn back the costs in any way, I'm just burning cash.

I would recommend treating the practical suggestions below like a pick 'n' mix, using what you like best and parking what you don't for later.

Podcast website

Once upon a time I'd have told you that a website is essential, but with podcasting these days, I'm not entirely sure that it is. My recommended services – Anchor and Libsyn – create branded and ready-made pages for you and it's possible these days to avoid entirely the need to create your own web presence. However, in the consultancy work I do with local businesses, I always recommend setting up a website – however basic it is – because this is the bit of online real estate that you own.

I call a website *the Mother Ship*, in that everything you do on the web – including social media – should feedback to it. If Facebook ever goes the way of Myspace, and Twitter takes a leaf out of Friends Reunited's book, all you'll be left with is a fading memory of likes and follows which are no longer any use to you. If you're in this podcasting game for the long term – and I hope that you are – having your own website will build resilience against future changes and give you a consistent place where listeners can always find you.

For instance, say you decide to change your podcast delivery service after a year; you'll have trained your listeners to go to a particular URL, but when you migrate between services, that weblink is likely to disappear. Your website will stay with you through good and bad, for better and for worse.

As already mentioned elsewhere in this book, Word-Press is my preferred service (check out my beginner's guide at PaulTeague.net/WP) and Wix is second-best, in that it's free and simple, but it's still built on somebody else's web property, so you don't own your site like you do with Word-Press. And to give the entire discussion some context, I would rather you just got your podcast launched before you worry too much about getting a website set up; do not let it become a block to you launching. It's good to have, and definitely something you should have once you're certain you're in podcasting for the long haul, but it's one of those things that can wait until you're ready to tackle it.

Show notes & SEO

As discussed elsewhere in this book, show notes provide a useful and valuable service to your listeners and are also an excellent source of SEO – Search Engine Optimisation. Show notes also provide an excellent opportunity to drive show listeners to your website, allowing them to interact with your affiliate promotions or personal products and services.

I hope you notice how everything that I've been telling you is linking up nicely now in a pitch-perfect pincer movement aimed at making the most out of your podcasting experience. The icing on the cake is to have all of this content on a website that you own, then it becomes your all-in-one marketing machine.

Show notes should include keywords related to your niche and topic, as this is what will help to generate steady organic web traffic over time; that's when people enter a word into Google that's related to your topic and your website or one of your web pages comes up in the results.

Episode titles

It's well worth deploying podcast episode titles strategically too as well-worded titles can really help with SEO and also with enticing new listeners to take your show out for a spin.

SEO is easy and something that we've already addressed; make sure that your episode titles incorporate the kind of words that your audience will be looking for.

Also, write headlines as if you're the person in charge of newspaper billboards; make them enticing without telling the entire story.

Finally, an excellent technique for tempting podcast listeners to try your show is to use simple solution-based headline styles, the type of headings that promise an easy solution to a problem in your niche. Examples of this technique include:

- 3/5/7/10 Ways to do XYZ
- 3/5/7/10 Simple Strategies for XYZ
- The 2-step/3-step/5-step Blueprint to XYZ
- How to Solve All your XYZ Problems in 3/5/7/10 Simple Steps

By the way, those number combinations work best too; there's something about the numbers I've used in those examples which generate a better response. The XYZ needs to incorporate SEO-related keywords. Here are some examples for specific topics;

- Episode X: *Ten Tips* to Help You **Start A Podcast** Today
- The *5-Step Process* for **Re-Shoe**ing a **Horse** Successfully Every Time
- *Three Ways* to Improve Your **Social Media** Skills Without Getting A Degree
- *Seven* of your most frequently asked **swimming** questions answered

Each of those headlines contains a keyword (bold), a number (in italics), and the promise of a simple solution to a problem in each niche. Now, you may cry *clickbait* at this point, but clickbait only applies if you don't deliver on your promise. The reason clickbait works is because it offers something that is enticing to the reader. We are promising something enticing, and so long as we deliver on that promise, we will retain our integrity and reputation.

Deployed correctly, careful wording on your episode titles not only helps to attract new listeners, it can also serve to create highly-trafficked and evergreen podcast shows which get consistently listened to, shared and commented on over time.

Strategic guest booking

I've mentioned this already earlier in the book, but it's worth a second mention to emphasise the importance of strategic guest booking when it comes to audience growth.

Say, Fred Blogs has thousands of readers for his car maintenance books and Freda Smith has hundreds of avid viewers of her car maintenance YouTube channel. It's early days for your podcast and you're only getting a hundred downloads per week.

By inviting Fred and Freda on as guests, not only do you get to access their wonderful knowledge and experience, you also get to skim off a little of their audience and introduce them to your show. And because they're in the same niche as you, you're a perfect fit. In addition, you'll also help Freda and Fred to grow their own audience. Interviews are great, evergreen content which is why so many people want to be a guest on podcasts. Take a look at the people who are ahead of you in your niche and start to make moves to invite them onto your show as a guest.

Social media & hashtags

When I started working on the internet, social media wasn't even a thing. If you wanted to find an audience, you had to start a blog or pay for Google Ads, that was pretty well it in those days. Social media is a gift to podcasters, allowing you to get your show distributed to millions of people throughout the world, usually at no cost.

There are five main channels to consider at present, unless you're targeting youngsters or young adults, in which case you're best asking somebody thirty years younger than me for advice. If your audience is made up of adults, here's what I recommend:

- Use LinkedIn if your podcast deals with a corporate or professional subject, for example, HR & Recruitment, accounting, business advice, marketing, veterinary services etc.
- Use Facebook if your audience can be targeted by topics or interests, for example, hobbies, music, books, TV, cinema etc.
- Use Twitter to source and connect with potential

guests for your podcast as well as using it strategically to find your audience.

- Use Instagram if you're able to create lots of strong images around what you do, for example, if you're an artist, crafter, farmer, skydiver etc (also consider using Pinterest).
- Use YouTube to syndicate your shows to a video-based channel if you use Libsyn – also use if you use a lot of 'how-to' demonstrations in your business.

I've done a lot of teaching around social media with local businesses and I usually advise them to pick one or two channels and to do them well before they get overwhelmed by trying to do everything at once. There was life before social media and there will be life after social media; use the channels that resonate best for you – even better if you're using them already – and become acquainted with the excellent, free service at Canva.com which will assist you in making and sharing eye-catching images for your podcast show.

Finally, without turning this book into a social media 'how-to', here are some useful tips to deploy:

- @mention show guests and products in your social media posts on Twitter, Facebook and LinkedIn.
- Add guest prospects to public lists in Twitter to get their initial attention. They get a notification letting them know they've been added to any public Twitter list. Make lists with great titles such as 'Bestselling authors' or 'Podcasting Experts'.

- Always use images with your social media posts, they get better engagement.
- Make your posts short and to the point – nobody likes 'War & Peace' unless you're sharing great 'how-to' information about an engaging personal story.
- Use a Facebook business page rather than your personal account for your podcast.
- Try to maintain a regular posting regime. You can post as often as you like on Twitter, no more than one - two times a day on a Facebook business page, and no more than one - two times a day on LinkedIn.
- Investigate the free social media scheduling tool at Buffer.com, it will help you to manage your time on social media better.

Email marketing

Email marketing is one of those skills that you'll need to learn eventually, but you can manage without in the early days of your podcast. However, if you listen to people who have managed to build up incredible web audiences online, most of them will tell you that they wish they'd started email marketing sooner. Please add this to the same list as building a website; it's essential, but please don't let it become a block to you getting your new podcast launched.

Email marketing is the second tier of your Mother Ship and helps you to further plug a vulnerability in social media channels. The problem with Facebook, Twitter and the like is that they're superb sources of potential listeners, but you don't own your likes and followers, you can't take them with you. Which means you own none of your data, it belongs to Facebook and Twitter.

I prefer to use social media as a rather superb conduit, allowing me to connect with hundreds, thousands and even millions of people all over the world, often at no cost to me whatsoever. However, I need to encourage them to share their email address with me if that essential contact information is to become mine; once I have your email address, I can contact you directly, even if Facebook goes the way of Myspace. When you have the email addresses of hundreds or thousands of podcast listeners, you are able to connect with them directly in their inbox, and that's a powerful thing.

The purpose of this book is not to teach you how to master the intricacies of email marketing, but to let you know it's a thing and that you should definitely investigate it further once you've got on top of the routines connected with your new podcast.

I'm going to recommend two email services to you; I've used them both and they offer fully-functional free tiers. They also provide step-by-step support and training, so make an excellent place for you to start if you're an email marketing newbie.

I use MailerLite in my own business; you can use it free when you get started and it still works out at excellent value when you're adding hundreds, then thousands of subscribers to your email marketing list. MailerLite has a lot of great features baked in, which makes it excellent value.

When I work with local businesses, they tend to be more familiar with Mailchimp, which also offers free access and will keep you going for a long time. Mailchimp is a good, solid service with plenty of support materials, so it makes a great place for you to get started with email marketing.

Finally, so that you can get to grips with the basics of email marketing, Tammi Labrecque's book *Newsletter Ninja* is a great place to start.

Channel listings

Make sure that your podcast is listed on as many channels as possible. Most podcast distribution services will offer a number of options. In my opinion, the basics are:

- Apple Podcasts
- Google Podcasts
- Spotify

In addition, you should also consider distributing your show to the following outlets:

- Stitcher
- TuneIn
- YouTube
- Facebook
- Instagram
- LinkedIn
- Twitter
- iHeartRadio

Encouraging reviews

Finally, in this section, you should do what you can to encourage reviews, as these provide social proof that your podcast is worth listening to. We expect you to tell us how great your show is, but when other people tell us, we tend to take more notice.

I think it's fair to say that Apple Podcasts reviews probably hold the most sway in this area, but you may also wish to encourage them on other channels.

One word about reviews: beware of sounding too needy or desperate when you ask for them, try to drop it in without making too big a meal out of it and sometimes – if you use an outro jingle – it might be less obtrusive if you make the request for reviews in the final jingle.

I picked up a great idea from either Colin Gray or Dave Jackson, I can't recall which, and I will pass it on here. It's an excellent strategy to create short *How to leave a review* videos (use Camtasia) or graphics (use Canva) as most people won't have a clue how to go about reviewing your show, even if they want to. I make these prominent on my website to make leaving those much-needed reviews as simple as possible.

Key points

- Social media is an excellent and free way to get the word out about your show. Pick a couple of channels to get things underway and consider using Buffer.com to assist with post scheduling.
- Don't forget the basics such as thinking about SEO on your show titles and show notes as well as coming up with enticing and distinctive podcast headlines.
- Consider very seriously getting a decent website for your podcast and building a list of email subscribers via a service like Mailchimp or MailerLite.

13

PODCASTING NEXT STEPS

By this stage you have everything you need to get podcasting. There are no excuses, you don't need that expensive piece of equipment before you get started, you don't need to invest in a £5000 course or mentorship programme; the only thing preventing you from getting started now is *you*. Sooner or later you're going to have to bite the bullet, take off the safety wheels, remove the net and make a leap of faith. It'll be great, believe me, the exhilaration of recording something at your kitchen table, letting it loose on the internet and then getting emails from people located all over the world never leaves you.

However, although I've given you more than enough information in this book to see you on your way, I'm a firm believer in lifelong learning and development, and I wouldn't want you to think for one moment that you now know everything there is to know about podcasting. Rather, I'd prefer you to make a start, try it on for size, do a couple of gentle stretching exercises then see where you could use a little more help or personal development. And that's where this chapter comes in.

I view my broadcasting career – including both radio and podcasting – as one of perpetual development. I don't think I've ever been completely happy with something I've done, though I have known that it's plenty good enough. In matters of the voice and ad-libbed presentation, it's unlikely it will ever be perfect. But you know, your audience won't mind, if they decide that they like you, they'll forgive a lot of foibles. Let's get those first podcast episodes released and then, when you're ready, check out some of these recommended next steps to keep you fresh, motivated and fully-engaged with the wonderful world of podcasting.

Books

I don't for one minute claim that this book contains every bit of learning there is on the process of podcasting. What you've got within these pages is my take, my personal view of the podcasting world. I hope it's informative and useful; I do believe I've managed to produce something new in the market, but you would do well to take some different views and perspectives into account too. You'll learn new tricks and tools from almost every podcaster that you encounter.

I've listed below some books which offer excellent next steps for further reading. I have followed the work of each author for some time and can vouch for them as a valuable source of trusted and sensible advice:

Podcaster: Joanna Penn

My notes: Joanna has been podcasting for many years and commands a huge audience and great respect in the indie author space. This book examines use of audio in a broader sense, but as a podcaster of ten years and counting, Joanna has some excellent insights into the medium.

Book: *Audio for Authors: Audiobooks, Podcasting, And Voice Technologies*
ISBN: 978-1913321239

Podcaster: Jon Cronshaw writing as J.L. Cronshaw

My notes: Jon is an author and podcasting friend and gave me the chance to beta read this book prior to release. He covers many elements which I do not, and it makes an ideal companion to this book.

Book: *Podcasting for Authors: How to Make and Publish a Podcast*
ISBN: 979-8601166430

Podcaster: Dave Jackson

My notes: Dave is my go-to source of excellent podcast advice. He's been podcasting for years and is greatly respected among podcasters.

Book: *Profit from Your Podcast: Proven Strategies to Turn Listeners into a Livelihood*
ISBN: 978-1621537724

Podcaster: John Lee Dumas

My notes: John is an amazing powerhouse of podcasting and every aspiring podcaster should have him on their radar. My claim to fame is that he recorded a jingle for my podcast in its early days.

Book: *Podcast Launch: How to Create & Launch Your Podcast: Plus FreePodcastCourse.com!*
ISBN: 978-1508418597

Podcaster: Colin Gray

My notes: Colin provides a safe, professional and experienced pair of hands when it comes to podcasting and can offer informed guidance on more complex equipment rigs and equipment.

Book: *How to Podcast: The Equipment, Strategy & Podcasting Skills You Need to Reach Your Audience: The book to guide you from Novice Podcaster to Confident Broadcaster*
ISBN: 978-0992690618

Podcasts on podcasting

As a podcast host yourself, you should definitely listen to podcasts. How else will you discover what works, what doesn't, and pick up great ideas for future developments?

Here is a short list of podcasts about podcasting which I recommend you check out:

Show title: School of Podcasting

Podcaster: Dave Jackson

My notes: Dave is my go-to source of information about podcasting. He's been producing and presenting shows for years, is a great host and provides all sorts of useful services for podcasters. I particularly like Dave's show because his advice is always practical and aimed at getting you started; he won't over-geek you or encourage you to spend money on equipment you don't need.

Show title: The Podcraft Podcast

Podcaster: Colin Gray

My notes: Colin is another of my preferred sources of quality podcasting information and his own podcast is well worth checking out. His back catalogue is packed with all sorts of fabulous information and I suggest a pick 'n' mix approach in the first instance, prioritising those topics which are most useful to you

Show title: The Feed

Podcaster: Libsyn

My notes: This is the podcast show produced by the team which provides my preferred podcast distribution service, Libsyn. It has a whole rack of previous episodes and I'd recommend you start by picking the topics which are most relevant to you.

Conferences

I will admit that I've never attended a podcasting conference, mainly because the dates have a nasty habit of clashing with other things that I have going on. However, I am a big fan of networking and learning events and recommend them highly to you.

This short list reflects UK and US venues and should be regarded as a starter kit. Do a Google search for *podcast events*; you'll soon discover that many more are available:

Event: Podcast Movement (US location)

My notes: Probably the biggest and best-known – this is the event which every podcaster needs to know about. On-demand recordings can be purchased if you can't attend in person.

Weblink: podcastmovement.com

Event: Pods Up North

My notes: This is my 'local' podcasting event and is a who's-who of UK podcasting talent.

Weblink: podsupnorth.com

Podcast mastermind groups

Courses and mentoring can provide huge benefits and I've been a frequent consumer of online courses and mastermind groups ever since I started working for myself. They usually come with a price tag attached, so they're not for everyone, but if you do want to take things to the next level, here's how you can get started:

Provider: Rob Moore

What's on offer? Podcast Media Masterclass at the offices in Peterborough, UK or a complete 'done-for-you' podcasting and editing service.

My notes: This is the podcasting mastermind group that I am a member of in the UK. Rob Moore presents a couple of podcasts of his own and has built an entire education and support service around it. The quarterly meetups are always packed with great guests and useful information.

Provider: Colin Gray

What's on offer? Podcasting courses, personal coaching and support, and resources and tools.

My notes: Colin has some great courses available and I particularly like the range of what's on offer. There are regular Q&A support sessions, so if you need ongoing 'hand-holding' this will be great for you.

Provider: Dave Jackson

What's on offer? Dave provides a variety of packages to suit every budget and requirement.

My notes: Dave's support is excellent, and I have used his services personally, paying him to review my show and give me feedback and tips.

Key points

- Get familiar with other podcast hosts who can take you to the next level.
- Conferences are an excellent way of networking and growing your podcasting circle and knowledge.
- Invest in yourself and your personal development; there's lots of help out there.

14

WHAT NEXT?

Congratulations, you made it to the end! We've covered a fair amount of ground; I'm betting you didn't even realise there was so much to podcasting when you set out on this journey. What I would emphasise, and I hoped you've picked up this sentiment throughout the book, is that you mustn't overcomplicate things. Don't spend more money than you can afford, keep it simple, release those first ten episodes and take it from there. I've given you everything you need to get started and to excel at your craft, the remainder is up to you.

Before I sign off and wish you well on your podcasting adventure, here are some final thoughts to see you on your way as you ride off into the sunset.

Networking

I can't place too high a value on the benefits of networking. It's great to meet up with fellow podcasters, share your tips and growing pains, and discover that you're not alone.

You don't have to attend faraway conferences or splash

out on expensive mastermind groups to achieve this. I recommend doing a bit of research, finding out who podcasts in your geographical area, and suggesting occasional meetups over coffee from time to time. You'll be amazed at how valuable these local meetups can be and how many solutions your podcasting colleagues will be able to suggest for any queries you have.

Review & improvement

Never sit back and think you know it all; podcasting is a journey and you can always improve in some way or learn a new trick that will enhance your process and technique.

I strongly recommend listening back to your own shows, even if only from time to time. I do this every week, consuming the show as a listener rather than as a host and producer. Always keep an open mind as to what's working, what is not and how you can make things better. And never forget the value of the audience; perhaps you could send them a survey and get their view on what they like best, what they'd like to see jettisoned and new features they'd like to see.

Changing format

Never hesitate to change your show format. Perhaps it doesn't feel right, maybe you sense it's getting stale, perhaps you just came up with a brilliant new feature that simply must be added to the mix as soon as possible.

When I worked in radio, we'd review show formats whenever the latest set of listening figures came in. We'd get breakdowns of listening during particular time slots, so if ever there was a drop-off in audience at a certain point in the show, we'd look at how we might tweak the format to prevent a switch-off point. You don't get data that's as detailed as that with a podcast, but the same principles apply. Always be looking for lulls in pace, parts of the show which don't mesh well and things that plain stand out, and not for a good reason. Feel free to mix it up, experiment, improve and refine.

Podburn

You're bound to hit the podburn zone at some time in your podcasting career. I certainly have. My week would be a lot clearer without having to record, edit and publish a show every week and, particularly when I'm under time pressure, I look at what can be pruned in my weekly schedule. The podcast always comes under scrutiny at these times.

I would caution responding to these feelings with a knee-jerk reaction. If you're feeling tired or jaded, this might be the time to deploy Colin Gray's excellent tactic of introducing seasons to your show, so that you can take regular breaks. Taking a break will allow you to reflect on your show away from the relentless pressures of having to turn out a new episode every week, and you will probably find some welcome clarity in that calmer time. Whenever I've taken a break, I always miss the routine of recording my weekly show; it's become an essential part of my own weekly routine.

Starting again

Sometimes it will be time to call it quits. Perhaps you chose the wrong topic and you have found that you limited yourself too much. In your initial enthusiasm, you may have committed to three weekly episodes only to find that you can't sustain that level of output. Perhaps you've come up with a new topic which inspires you more or maybe something came up in your life and it's just not practical any more.

If you need to give up and walk away for a time – or if you want to start again – that's absolutely fine. The great thing about podcasts is that they are a permanent record of the work you did, whether you released 5, 25, 105 or 5000 shows. You don't need to delete anything, just leave it online and your show will continue to find an audience.

I recently started listening to a podcast where the hosts had walked away after hundreds of episodes in 2015 to deal with some issues which life had thrown their way. Three years later, the time was right for them to pick up the show again. It got a new title, different music and off they went again. It's like they were never away, they just picked up where they left off. Never be afraid to stop and start over; just take a little time before deciding to end things to consider if it's just a break that you need.

Podcast statistics

Get used to looking at your download statistics and, if your podcast distributor provides this service, get excited about how many countries your show is consumed in. Unless you get very lucky or have an existing audience, podcast growth will be slow at first. Don't get too downhearted if the numbers seem low, it can be a hard slog sometimes.

Instead of correlating feelings of success or failure with the number of downloads that you get, instead, ask yourself if you've managed to connect with and serve an audience, however small. You'll get a sense of this from email and social media messages as well as reviews. If you're serving even a small and enthusiastic crowd of people, you're doing okay, you're not wasting your time.

If you search online, you'll be able to discover how many downloads the average podcast gets. But in a survey that was recent at the time of publication, the Libsyn podcast The Feed revealed that you're in the top 50% of podcasts if your episodes get 136 downloads or more within 30 days of release. That's a very achievable number for most people, so stay with it and be patient, your time will come. And if you reach the top 1% of podcasts with more than 36,000 downloads within 30 days of release, you should be writing a book like this, not reading it.

My resources & tools

To enable me to keep this book up to date without having to release new versions of it every five minutes, I have added weblinks to the accompanying website for this book at Paul-Teague.net/POD. I'll keep that updated as information changes and add in anything else that might be useful. But that weblink is where you'll find direct links to everything I mention in this book, plus plenty of extra bits.

Final words

Thank you for reading this book. I hope it will serve you well in that it has given you everything you need to start a podcast, but also to help you on your journey beyond the release of those first episodes, to the stage where you're a veteran of 50, 100 or even 500 podcast episodes.

I'll finish off where I began. I have never known a medium like it; podcasting has allowed me to connect more closely with listeners than radio ever did, and I predict great things for the industry in the years ahead. There's nothing quite like podcasting and, if you catch the bug, I'm certain that it will serve you well for many years to come whether you use it as a hobby, a business or both.

Good luck with your new podcast show and I wish you many happy years of production, recording and publication; an amazing audio adventure awaits!

ABOUT THE AUTHOR

Hi, I'm Paul Teague and I'm a non-fiction, thriller and science fiction writer from the UK.

I write non-fiction as P. Teague, thrillers as Paul J. Teague and science fiction as Paul Teague.

I'm a former broadcaster and journalist with the BBC, but I have also worked as a primary school teacher, a disc jockey, a shopkeeper, a waiter and a sales rep.

Let's get connected!
https://paulteague.net

Printed in Great Britain
by Amazon

81403931R00130